1

Wide Angle

WORKBOOK

NANCY JORDAN

OXFORD
UNIVERSITY PRESS

OXFORD
UNIVERSITY PRESS

198 Madison Avenue
New York, NY 10016 USA

Great Clarendon Street, Oxford, OX2 6DP,
United Kingdom

Oxford University Press is a department of the University of Oxford. It furthers the University's objective of excellence in research, scholarship, and education by publishing worldwide. Oxford is a registered trade mark of Oxford University Press in the UK and in certain other countries

© Oxford University Press 2019

ISBN: 978 0 19 452842 9

Printed in China
This book is printed on paper from certified and well-managed sources.

ACKNOWLEDGMENTS

Back cover photograph: Oxford University Press building/David Fisher

Illustrations by: 5W Infographics pp 16; Arunas Kacinska/Eye Candy Illustration pp. 15,19; John Jay pp. 53.

Video by: Mannic Productions pp: 12, 26, 47, 54, 61, 68, 75.

The Publishers would like the thank the following for their kind permission to reproduce photographs and other copyright material: **123rf:** pp. 16 (table/Andrew Mayovskyy), 23 (family/Lucky Business), 27 (woman/Nenad Aksic), 45 (beach/Tatiana Popova). **Alamy:** pp 30 (scientist/Rafe Swan), 30 (author/Sue Andrews), 31 (traffic/Global Warming Imags), 36 (athlete/DPA Picture Alliance), 39 (student/Hero Images Inc.), 41 (student/Hero Images Inc.), 42 (Phelps/DPA Picture Alliance Archive), 45 (Boy/ Dmitriy Shironosov), 45 (desert/Blickwinkel), 45 (skiing/Tetra Images), 46 (snow/ Blend Images), 48 (old guy/US photography), 54 (Birthday/Gallo Images), 55 (old car/ Tom Wood), 62 (park/Givaga), 67 (store/Alex Segre), 67 (tv screen/MBI), 69 (climbing/ aurora photos), 74 (chess/Andor Budjdoso), 80 (laptop/Robin Beckham/BEEPstock), 82 (invitation/Yay Media Sa), 4 (soccer ball/John Baran), 11 (wheelchair/BSIP SA), 16 (refrigerator/Vladislav Kochelaesvkly), 16 (bed/Zoonar GmbH). **Blink:** pp. Cover & photo opener: Krisanne Johnson, 52 (sneakers/Krisanne Johnson), 76 (Classroom/ Edu Bayer), 30 (accordion/Nadia Shira Cohen), 51 (Girl in hat/Krisanne Johnson), **Getty:** pp. 7 (man/Popperfoto), 17 (french quarter/Toby Adamson), 30 (Yayoi Kusama/ Jeremy Sutton-Hibbert), 32 (pretzel/Dallosto), 43 (women/Geber86), 60 (Donuts/ Martine Mouchy), 67 (cave/Giordano Caprioni), 67 (ocean/Jonathan Kingston), 70 (Oscar Wilde/Alfred Ellis & Walery/Stringer), 74 (designer/Porta Images), 74 (runner/ Michael Steele), 74 (rain/Radius Images), 74 (wheelchhair/ V. Iakobchuk), 83 (boy at window/Laflor) **Shutterstock:** pp. 3 (cellist/urbazon), 3 (artist/DnDavis), 4 (tacos/ zoryanchik), 4 (Danica Patrick/Daniel Hurlimann), 4 (mini cooper/Grisha Bruev), 4 (dollar/Anton Watman), 5 (handshake/Rawpixel.com), 6 (woman/Antonio Diaz), 10 (man shopping/Iakov Filimonov), 13 (Restaurant/Raw Pixel.com), 14 (moon/Vovan), 16 (sofa/Bluehand), 22 (3men/SydaProductions), 24 (M.Zuckerberg/Frederic Legrand - COMEO), 30 (passenger/Andrey Yurlov), 32 (bed/India Picture), 32 (sportscar/Ermess), 32 (guitairst/Anastasia Vavilina), 32 (phone/Nebjosa Markvic), 32 (sunglasses/Guzel Studio), 32 (bed/M. Ali Khan), 32 (tennis/Fresnel), 34 (Eiffel Tower/Claudia K), 38 (woman/Monkey Business Images), 51 (woman in dress/Lapina), 51 (man in suit/ ASDF_MEDIA), 51 (woman in skirt/ASDF_MEDIA), 51 (family/Antonio Diaz), 53 (balloons/Business Stock), 53 (camera/OsorioArtist), 53 (basketball/Wave Break Media,) 53 (airplane/Frank Peters), 53 (computer/mirtmirt), 57 (café/Africa Studio), 59 (Ice Cream/Oleksandra Naumenko), 60 (mac n' cheese/Igor Dutina), 60 (fruit/ baibaz), 60 (vegetables/Maks Narodenko), 60 (fish/Africa Studio), 60 (cake/Studio Romantic), 66 (forest/ER_09), 67 (village/Jeni Foto), 69 (women in musuem, Iokov Filimoov), 74 (Taj Mahal/Hung Chung Chi). **Superstock:** pp. 30 (driver/Caia Images),

Authentic Content Provided by Oxford Reference

The author and publisher are grateful to those who have given permission to reproduce the following extracts and adaptations or copyright material:

p.3 Adapted from *A Guide to Countries of the World* edited by Christopher Riches and Peter Stalker. Copyright Oxford University Press, 2016. http://www.oxfordreference. com/view/10.1093/acref/9780191803000.001.0001/acref-9780191803000

p. 7 Patrick McGoohan, George Markstein and David Tomblin in *Oxford Essential Quotations (5th ed.)* edited by Susan Ratcliffe. Copyright Oxford University Press 2017 http://www.oxfordreference.com/view/10.1093/acref/9780191843730.001.0001/q-oro-ed5-00006942?rskey=pLmgxq&result=1

p.10 Adapted from *A Dictionary of Environment and Conservation (3 ed.)* by Chris Park and Michael Allaby. Copyright Oxford University Press 2017 http://www.oxfordreference. com/view/10.1093/acref/9780191826320.001.0001/acref-9780191826320-e-8748?rskey=1XX2al&result=6

p.14 Buddy De Sylva and Lew Brown in *Oxford Dictionary of Modern Quotations (7th ed.)* edited by Elizabeth Knowles Copyright Oxford University Press 2009 http://www. oxfordreference.com/view/10.1093/acref/9780199237173.001.0001/q-author-00001-00000959?rskey=Nps54E&result=1

p.17 Adapted from *The Oxford Encyclopedia of American Cultural and Intellectual History,* edited by Joan Shelley Rubin and Scott E. Casper. Copyright Oxford University Press 2016 http://www.oxfordreference.com/view/10.1093/acref/9780199764358.001.0001/ acref-9780199764358-e-480?rskey=qBS0ZY&result=2

p.21 J.H. Payne in *Oxford Essential Quotations (5th ed.)* edited by Susan Ratcliffe Copyright Oxford University Press 2017 http://www.oxfordreference. com/view/10.1093/acref/9780191843730.001.0001/q-oro-ed5-00008225?rskey=VZMVN5&result=3

p.24 Adapted from *A Dictionary of Computer Science,* edited by Andrew Butterfield and Gerard Ekembe Ngondi. Copyright Oxford University Press 2016 http:// www.oxfordreference.com/view/10.1093/acref/9780199688975.001.0001/acref-9780199688975-e-6759?rskey=qdhSYL&result=1

p.28 Amos Bronson Alcott in *Oxford Essential Quotations (5th ed.)* edited by Susan Ratcliffe. Copyright Oxford University Press 2017 http://www. oxfordreference.com/view/10.1093/acref/9780191843730.001.0001/q-oro-ed5-00011946?rskey=cElGSt&result=2

p.31 Adapted from *A Dictionary of Public Health,* edited by John Last. Copyright Oxford University Press 2007 http://www.oxfordreference.com/view/10.1093/ acref/9780195160901.001.0001/acref-9780195160901-e-3959?rskey=Aynel4&result=1

p. 35 Peg Bracken in *Oxford Dictionary of Humorous Quotations (5th ed.)* edited by Gyles Brandreth. Copyright Oxford University Press 2013 http://www. oxfordreference.com/view/10.1093/acref/9780199681365.001.0001/q-subject-00008-00000286?rskey=RMxnjR&result=1

p.38 Adapted from *A Dictionary of Human Resource Management (3rd ed.)* by Edmund Heery and Mike Noon. Copyright Oxford University Press 2017 http://www. oxfordreference.com/view/10.1093/acref/9780191827822.001.0001/acref-9780191827822-e-1721?rskey=1itjf5&result=4

p. 42 Michael Phelps in *Oxford Essential Quotations, (5th ed.)* edited by Susan Ratcliffe. Copyright Oxford University Press 2017 http://www. oxfordreference.com/view/10.1093/acref/9780191843730.001.0001/q-oro-ed5-00008298?rskey=DLyO9e&result=1

p.45 Adapted from *A Dictionary of Public Health* edited by John M. Last. Copyright Oxford University Press 2013 http://www.oxfordreference.com/ view/10.1093/acref/9780195160901.001.0001/acref-9780195160901-e-4059?rskey=Wwsjav&result=3

p. 49 Michelle Obama in *Oxford Essential Quotations (5th ed)* edited by Susan Ratcliffe Copyright Oxford University Press 2017 http://www.oxfordreference.com/ view/10.1093/acref/9780191843730.001.0001/q-oro-ed5-00016286

p.52 Adapted from *A Dictionary of Sports Studies* by Alan Thomlinson. Copyright Oxford University Press 2010. http://www.oxfordreference.com/view/10.1093/ acref/9780199213818.001.0001/acref-9780199213818-e-802?rskey=iJ7ZJG&result=1

p. 56 L. P. Hartley in *Oxford Dictionary of Quotations (8th ed.)* edited by Elizabeth Knowles. Copyright Oxford University Press 2014 http://www.oxfordreference. com/view/10.1093/acref/9780199668700.001.0001/q-author-00010-00001523?rskey=XclqYz&result=2

p.59 Adapted from *Food and Fitness: A Dictionary of Diet and Exercise (2nd ed.)* by Michael Kent. Copyright Oxford University Press 2016 http://www.oxfordreference. com/view/10.1093/acref/9780191803239.001.0001/acref-9780191803239-e-404?rskey=SkU0Jw&result=10

p.63 Sydney Smith in *Oxford Essential Quotations (5th ed.)* edited by Susan Ratcliffe. Copyright Oxford University Press 2017 http://www. oxfordreference.com/view/10.1093/acref/9780191843730.001.0001/q-oro-ed5-00005620?rskey=vuoY9x&result=1

p. 66 Adapted from *A Guide to Countries of the World (4ed)* by Christopher Riches and Peter Stalker. Copyright Oxford University Press 2016 http://www.oxfordreference. com/view/10.1093/acref/9780191803000.001.0001/acref-9780191803000-e-0052?rskey=RfZRSK&result=10

p.70 Oscar Wilde in *Oxford Essential Quotations (5th ed.)* edited by Susan Ratcliffe. Copyright Oxford University Press 2017 http://www. oxfordreference.com/view/10.1093/acref/9780191843730.001.0001/q-oro-ed5-00004973?rskey=27njnG&result=1

p. 74 Adapted from *The Oxford Companion to the Body,* by Colin Blakemore and Sheila Jennett. Oxford University Press 2003 http://www.oxfordreference. com/view/10.1093/acref/9780198524038.001.0001/acref-9780198524038-e-868?rskey=vDEMlL&result=3

p.77 Malala Yousafzai in *Oxford Essential Quotations (5th ed.)* edited by Susan Ratcliffe. Copyright Oxford University Press 2017 http://www. oxfordreference.com/view/10.1093/acref/9780191843730.001.0001/q-oro-ed5-00017266?rskey=WhawOt&result=2

p. 80 Adapted from *The Oxford Encyclopedia of American Intellectual and Cultural History,* by Joan Shelley Rubin and Scott E. Casper. Copyright Oxford University Press 2013 http://www.oxfordreference.com/view/10.1093/acref/9780199764358.001.0001/acref-9780199764358-e-524?rskey=LkqAaU&result=1

p.84 Philander Chase Johnson in *Oxford Dictionary of Quotations (8th ed.)* edited by Elizabeth Knowles. Copyright Oxford University Press 2014 http://www. oxfordreference.com/view/10.1093/acref/9780199668700.001.0001/q-author-00010-00001781?rskey=CBnLZn&result=1

Contents

1 Self

The verb *be*: Positive and subject pronouns ▶1.1

1 Complete the sentences. Use *am*, *is*, or *are*.

1 Kaito _____ from Tokyo.

2 I _____ from Japan, too.

3 We _____ both Japanese.

4 Hanna and Emilia _____ from Germany.

5 They _____ German.

6 You _____ Mexican.

2 Complete the sentences. Use *am*, *is*, or *are*.

1 My mother works in a hospital. She _____ a doctor.

2 I _____ an international student in Paris!

3 People speak German in Austria. It _____ an official language.

4 My family lives in the United States. We _____ from Poland.

5 My brother teaches math. He _____ a good teacher.

6 You study a lot. You _____ a great student.

Questions with *be* ▶1.2

3 Complete the questions with the correct word.

Are	How	Is	What	What	Where

1 _____ is your first name?

2 _____ are you from?

3 _____ is your phone number?

4 _____ old are you?

5 _____ you a student?

6 _____ your English teacher nice?

4 Answer the questions in Exercise 3 with true answers about yourself.

1 _____

2 _____

3 _____

4 _____

5 _____

6 _____

5 Complete the conversations.

1 A: _____ you American?

   B: No, _____. I'm Australian.

2 A: _____ she from Peru?

   B: No, _____. She's Brazilian.

3 A: _____ they from Vietnam?

   B: Yes, _____.

4 A: _____ your dad American?

   B: No, _____. He's British.

5 A: _____ he from Brazil?

   R: Yes, _____.

Be: Negative ▶1.3

6 Choose the correct form of *be*.

1 Frida Kahlo *isn't* / *aren't* from Brazil. She's from Mexico.

2 She *is* / *isn't* a famous artist.

3 Lionel Messi plays soccer in Spain, but he *isn't* / *is* from Argentina.

4 They *are* / *aren't* British. They're from London.

5 We *isn't* / *aren't* from the United States. We're from Canada.

7 Complete the sentences with the correct negative form of *be*.

1 My name _____ Paul.

2 I _____ Brazilian.

3 We _____ scientists.

4 Anna _____ famous.

5 They _____ students here.

6 You _____ from Egypt.

VOCABULARY DEVELOPMENT:
Nationalities ▶1.1

1 Use the endings to complete the chart with nationalities for the countries in the box. Two are irregular.

China	Japan	Russia	the United Kingdom
France	~~Mexico~~	Spain	the United States
India	Poland		

Mexican	-an
	-ese
	-ish
	-n
	irregular

2 Complete the sentences using the nationalities from Exercise 1.

1 I study in the United States, but I am from Mexico.
  I am _Mexican_.

2 My family lives in Russia. We are _____.

3 My mother is from Japan, but my father is from Spain.
  He is _____.

4 I live in the United Kingdom. My parents are from India. They are _____.

5 My father is from the United Kingdom, but my mom is from China. She is _____.

6 My son works in Russia, but we are from Poland. We are _____.

7 I am from Japan, but I live in Spain. I am _____.

Numbers 1–20 ▶1.2

3 Match the numbers.

1	6	a	three
2	18	b	eleven
3	9	c	six
4	11	d	four
5	16	e	nine
6	4	f	eighteen
7	5	g	sixteen
8	3	h	five

4 Write the numbers.

1	seven	_7_	5	two	___
2	nineteen	___	6	ten	___
3	twelve	___	7	one	___
4	fifteen	___	8	seventeen	___

5 Write the numbers from Exercise 4 in order.
  1, 2, _____

Jobs ▶1.3

6 Unscramble the letters to make job names.

1 ruohat   a _____
2 tisenisct   s _____
3 crtodo   d _____
4 crtao   a _____
5 sattri   a _____
6 smbanusisen   b _____

7 Complete the sentences with a word from the box.

artist   author   musician   scientist   soccer player

1 Yayoi Kusamas my favorite _____. She makes lots of different kinds of art.

2 Luis Suárez is a great _____. He plays in Spain, but he is from Uruguay.

3 Jane Goodall is a famous _____. She studies chimps in Africa.

4 I love piano music. Mozart is my favorite _____, but I listen to pop music, too.

5 Amy Tan is a great writer. She is the _____ of my favorite book.

1 Read the student profiles. Where are Petr and Maria from?

Spotlight on International Students

Meet some of our new students from around the world!

◀**Petr Novak**

My name is Petr. I'm a musician from Prague. It's the capital city of the Czech Republic. I speak Czech. It's the official language, but I also speak English. Many people from the Czech Republic speak English. My parents speak it, too. Our currency is the Czech koruna. We also call it the crown.

Maria Jones ▶

My name is Maria. I study art in Mexico City. It is the capital city in Mexico, but I am from Guadalajara. My mom is Mexican. She is a teacher. My dad is American, and he is a teacher, too. People speak Spanish in Mexico. I speak Spanish and English. Mexico's official currency is the peso.

—Adapted from *A Guide to Countries of the World*, 4th ed., by Christopher Riches and Peter Stalker

2 Read the student profiles again. Then complete the sentences.

1 The official language of the Czech Republic is ___Czech___.

2 The currency of the Czech Republic is the _____.

3 Petr speaks _____ and _____.

4 Maria studies _____.

5 Maria speaks _____ and _____.

6 Maria's dad is not Mexican. He is _____.

3 Look at the kinds of information in the profiles. Which is about the country and which is about the person? Write *C* for country and *P* for person.

1 job   ___P___

2 studies   _____

3 official language   _____

4 nationality of parents   _____

5 currency   _____

6 capital city   _____

REAL-WORLD READING

READING SKILL: Recognizing nouns and pronouns ▶1.1

4 Match the sentence in A with the sentence in B.

A

1 I'm a musician from Prague. ____

2 I speak Czech. ____

3 Many people from the Czech Republic speak English. ____

4 Our currency is the Czech koruna. ____

B

a We call it the crown, too.

b My parents speak it, too.

c It's the official language.

d It's the capital city of the Czech Republic.

5 Find two more nouns and their pronouns in Maria's profile on page 3 of this workbook.

6 Find the noun that goes with the pronoun.

1 The dollar is American. It is green and white.

2 I love Mini Coopers. They are fast!

3 I like soccer. Brazil is famous for it.

4 Tacos are Mexican. They are delicious!

5 Danica Patrick is American. She is a race car driver.

REAL-WORLD ENGLISH: Greetings and introductions ▶1.4

1 Complete the dialogue from Scene 1 of the video with words from the box.

are	good	hello	meet	too

Max: ¹_____. Are you Andy?

Andy: Yeah! ²_____ you Max?

Max: Yeah. Ah…³_____ to ⁴_____ you, roommate!

Andy: Yeah, you ⁵_____.

Andy: Here…Let me…

Max: Thanks!

2 Complete the dialogue from Scene 2 of the video.

good morning	how's it going	what	what's up
how are	nice	what's up	where

Kevin: Hey! Uh, is this college writing?

Max: Yep! ¹_____? I'm Max. ²_____ to meet you.

Kevin: Kevin. Yeah, you too.

Max: Oh, there's my roommate!

Kevin: Andy! Hey…³_____?

Andy: Hey! ⁴_____ you doing?

Kevin: Good, uh, yeah. So, uh, ⁵_____ are you from, Max?

Max: From England. ⁶_____ about you?

Kevin: Minnesota.

Andy: We're both from Minnesota. We're old friends.

Prof Lopez: ⁷_____. My name's Karen Lopez, and I'm your professor.

Max/Andy: Good morning!

Kevin: Hey! ⁸_____?

3 Look at the picture, and read the conversation. Answer the questions.

Man 1:   Hi, Mr. Smith. I'm Mr. Jones. It's very nice to meet you. We
         are excited to meet one of our son's professors.

Man 2:   Hey, what's up?

1 Man 2's greeting *is / isn't* good.
2 Man 1's greeting *is / isn't* good.
3 This *is /isn't* a relaxed conversation.
4 Man 2 *does / does not* introduce himself.
5 This *is / is not* their first meeting.

4 Rewrite any parts of the conversation that aren't good.

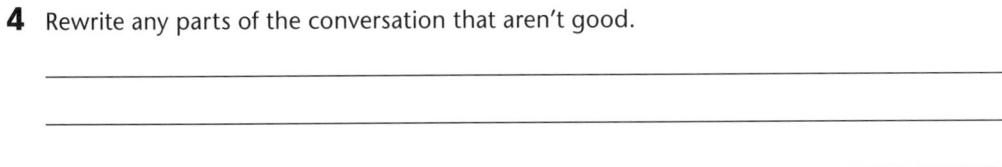

_____

_____

UNIT REVIEW: Podcast

 GO ONLINE to listen to the podcast from the Unit Review.

1 🔊 Listen to the Unit Review Podcast. Choose *True* or *False*.

		True	False
1	The man and the woman are good friends.	☐	☐
2	The woman is an artist.	☐	☐
3	The book is about Facebook.	☐	☐
4	The woman says identity is who you are.	☐	☐
5	The woman says identity is where you love and dream.	☐	☐

2 🔊 Listen again and complete the conversation.

A: Hi. My ¹_____ is James Marshall and I'm from *Book-TV*. Rebecca Blunt is here ²_____.

B: Hi, James. ³_____ to meet you.

A: Nice to meet you. Rebecca, you're the author of a popular ⁴_____, *My Identities*.

B: Yes, it's a book about identity.

A: For you, identity isn't Facebook. What is identity?

B: Identity is who you are. It isn't ⁵_____ you are. That is what you ⁶_____ on Facebook.

A: What is your identity?

B: I explain my identity with a quote, "⁷_____ is where the heart is."

A: Why is that?

B: Home is where you love and dream. That is identity to me—the places and people you ⁸_____ and your ⁹_____.

LISTENING SKILL: Understanding content words in speech ▶1.3

3 🔊 Listen to these sentences from the podcast. Underline the content words in each sentence.

1 I'm from *Book-TV*. (one content word)
2 It's a book about identity. (two content words)
3 For you, identity isn't Facebook. (two content words)
4 Identity is who you are. (two content words)
5 Home is where you love and dream. (three content words)

DISCUSSION BOARD PREPARATION

4 Look at the Unit 1 Review Discussion Point. Read the questions in the prompt. Then read the reply. What quote describes the writer?

_____

5 Label the part of the reply that answers Question 1 from the prompt. Then label the parts that answer Question 2 and Question 3.

_____

Unit 1 Review Discussion Point

Answer the questions in a post.
1　Read the quote. What does it mean?
　"I am not a number, I am a free man!"
　—Number Six, *The Prisoner* (TV series 1967–68), selected from *Oxford Essential Quotation*, 5ᵗʰ ed., edited by Susan Ratcliffe
2　Write a quote that describes you.
3　Why does this quote describe you?

Latest: Juan Ruiz
This quote means that identity is not the numbers the government gives you.
　A quote that describes me is, "Dream the impossible dream." This quote describes me because I have my dream job. I am an author. It is not impossible, but it is hard to be an author. That is why the quote describes me.

6 Overall, did the writer answer all the questions? If yes, explain. If no, what can he change?

_____

_____

7 Review the rubric. Use the rubric to give a score for the reply.
Give points: 0 (not successful)–10 (successful).

Writing a Discussion Board Post	Points
The post answers the questions clearly and completely.	
The post uses the verb *be* correctly.	
The post uses subject pronouns correctly.	
The post shows careful thinking about the topic.	
Sentences are complete and have correct punctuation.	
The post is long enough (50–60 words).	
Total	

WRITE YOUR POST

8 Read the quote. What does it mean? Write a quote that describes you. Why does this quote describe you? Write your post for the discussion board.

 "I am not a free man!"
—Number Six, *The Prisoner*
(TV series 1967–68), selected from
Oxford Essential Quotations, 5ᵗʰ ed.,
edited by Susan Ratcliffe

9 Use the rubric from Exercise 7 to score your post. Then improve your post.

Go online to add your comments to the discussion board.

2 Things

Singular and plural nouns ▶2.1

1 Write the plural form of the nouns.

1 woman _____
2 key _____
3 person _____
4 phone _____
5 man _____
6 teacher _____
7 child _____
8 ticket _____

2 Correct the mistakes with *a* or *an*. One sentence is correct.

1 Those are a cheap phones.
Those are cheap phones.

2 That's fun game.
_____

3 Gifts are great!
_____

4 I have an picture of my house.
_____

5 Bag is a nice gift.
_____

6 I have a idea!
_____

Demonstrative adjectives and pronouns ▶2.2

3 Read the sentences. Circle the correct words.

1 *This / These* are my keys.
2 *That / These* picture is interesting.
3 Is *this / those* your phone?
4 *That / Those* old cars are really big!
5 *That / These* bags are ugly.
6 *This / Those* is Jack's wallet.

4 Look at the chart, and complete the sentences with *this, that, these,* or *those*.

Near the speaker	Not near the speaker
Dasan	houses
keys	car
glasses	book

1 _____ is my brother, Dasan.
2 _____ houses are beautiful.
3 Are _____ your keys?
4 _____ is a nice car.
5 _____ glasses are expensive.
6 _____ is an interesting book.

Possessive 's and possessive adjectives ▶2.3

5 Write the words in the correct columns.

Arvind's	his	my sister's	she	we
he	I	our	their	you
her	my	Rosa's	they	your

Subject pronouns	Possessive adjectives	Possessive 's

6 Complete the sentences with the correct possessive adjectives.

1 They are brothers. _____ last name is Park.
2 We love soccer. _____ favorite team is Real Madrid.
3 She is an English teacher. _____ students are from many different countries.
4 Please email me. _____ address is webster31@mailinator.com.
5 You're a new student, right? What is _____ name?
6 He's from Brazil. _____ first language is Portuguese.

7 Write the apostrophes in the correct place.

1 Those are Marias glasses.
2 Ryans keys are in his car.
3 This is my sisters son.
4 Are these Nicks book?
5 Your friends pictures are beautiful. I can't believe she went to Italy.

VOCABULARY DEVELOPMENT:
Numbers 21–101 ▶2.1

1 Write the numbers.

1 forty-three   ____

2 one hundred and one   ____

3 twenty-seven   ____

4 seventy-five   ____

5 thirty-eight   ____

6 eighty-nine   ____

7 ninety-two   ____

8 fifty-six   ____

9 sixty-four   ____

10 a hundred   ____

2 Find the numbers in the sentences. Write them in words.

1 This bag is (49) dollars. _forty-nine_

2 My grandmother is 82 years old. _____

3 We have 25 students in my English class. _____

4 My favorite soccer player's number is 37. _____

5 I am 31 years old. _____

6 My favorite number is 63. _____

7 The basketball game is on channel 54. _____

8 Those concert tickets are 100 dollars. _____

Adjectives ▶2.2

3 Unscramble the letters to make adjectives.

1 clbka

    b _____

2 mslal

    s _____

3 ewn

    n _____

4 yulg

    u _____

5 thwie

    w _____

6 albuieuft

    b _____

4 Match each word in *A* with its opposite in *B*.

A   B

____ 1 ugly   a white

____ 2 big   b small

____ 3 new   c beautiful

____ 4 black   d old

5 Read the sentences. Choose the correct words.

1 Fifteen books are in his bag. His bag is *big / small*!

2 Wow, your bag is *ugly / beautiful*! I'd like one, too. Is it Peruvian?

3 *Casablanca* is on TV. It's my favorite movie! It's in black and *blue / white*.

4 This cell phone is $20. It's from 2008, so it's *new / old*.

5 I don't like that house. It's *ugly / beautiful*.

6 His house is *big / small*. It has three rooms.

7 I like *black / white* coffee, with no milk.

8 That's a nice bag. Is it *new / old*?

Personal items ▶2.3

6 Find the spelling mistake in each word. Write the correct spelling.

1 cell fone   _____

2 glases   _____

3 pictur   _____

4 cumputer   _____

5 mony   _____

6 keye   _____

7 Complete the sentences with the correct word from Exercise 6.

1 This is a _____ of my friend, Laura.

2 My _____ is in my wallet.

3 Is this the _____ to your house?

4 Your new _____ are beautiful!

5 What is your _____ number?

6 That _____ is expensive. It's $2,500!

VOCABULARY

1 Read the article. What is "clutter"?

Stop the Clutter!

Justin Harrington is often late to work. Why? He can't find his keys, his phone, or his sunglasses. Justin's home is "cluttered"—there are a lot of things in it. Many people have this problem!

Elsa Martinez is the author of *Goodbye Clutter!* Her book gives some interesting numbers:

- The typical British ten-year-old has 238 toys, but only plays with 12 every day.
- Shopping is the favorite activity of 93% of American girls.
- People in the United States buy 40% of the world's toys, but have only 3% of the world's children.
- Most people wear 20% of their clothes 80% of the time.
- Americans spend $1.2 trillion dollars ($1,200,000,000,000) a year on things they don't need.

Martinez says, "People don't need many things. It is better to have the things we need, and nothing more."

—adapted from *A Dictionary of Environment and Conservation*, 3rd ed., by Chris Park and Michael Allaby

2 Choose the correct answers.

1 Why is Justin often late to work?

a He can't find things.   b His car is old.

2 What is Justin's problem?

a He doesn't like his job.   b He has clutter in his home.

3 What is the name of Elsa Martinez's book?

a *Goodbye Clutter*   b *Stop the Clutter*

4 What is Elsa Martinez's book about?

a how to say goodbye   b stopping clutter

3 Choose *True* or *False*.

	True	False
1 Justin has a job.	☐	☐
2 Justin doesn't have many things in his home.	☐	☐
3 Many people have clutter in their homes.	☐	☐
4 American girls like to shop.	☐	☐
5 Elsa Martinez likes clutter.	☐	☐

READING SKILL: Recognizing numbers in a text ▶2.1

4 Read the article again. Find the numbers in the article, and write them below.

1 _____

2 _____

3 _____

4 _____

5 _____

6 _____

7 _____

8 _____

9 _____

5 Write the numbers next to the things.

1 _____ age of British child

2 _____ trillions of dollars

3 _____ percent of American girls

4 _____ percent of the world's toys that Americans buy

5 _____ percent of the world's children that are American

6 _____ % of their clothes Americans often wear

7 _____ toys a British child plays with every day

6 Look at readings on pages 17 and 24 of this workbook. Write the numbers you find. Write the things next to the numbers.

Workbook page	Number	Thing
17		
17		
24		
24		
24		
24		
24		
24		

REAL-WORLD ENGLISH: Being polite to strangers ▶2.4

1 Complete the dialogue from the video with words from the box.

excuse me	I'd like	please	sorry	thanks

Andy: ¹_____?

Sarah: Oh, hi there. ²_____ about that. How can I help you?

Andy: ³_____ one small black coffee, uh, and a regular tea, ⁴_____.

Sarah: That is three dollars and seventy-nine cents.

Andy: Oh, no! My wallet's at home!

Max: Oh! No problem. It's on me.

Sarah: One dollar and twenty-one cents is your change.

Max: ⁵_____!

2 Read the conversation. Which lines are polite? Which lines are not polite?

			Polite	Not polite
1	Customer:	Hey!	☐	☑
2	Server:	Yes? How can I help you?	☐	☐
3	Customer:	I want a large tea.	☐	☐
4	Server:	We don't have tea.	☐	☐
5	Customer:	Oh. Give me a coffee.	☐	☐
6	Server:	Sure. That's two dollars and fifty cents. Here you are.	☐	☐
7	Customer:	Thank you.	☐	☐
8	Server:	Yes.	☐	☐

3 Rewrite the lines that aren't polite.

Line	Polite rewrite

UNIT REVIEW: Podcast

 Go online and listen to the podcast from the Unit Review.

1 🔊 Listen to the podcast. Choose *True* or *False*.

	True	False
1 Kevin Shum is a scientist.	☐	☐
2 Buying things makes people very happy.	☐	☐
3 Being with friends makes people a little bit happy.	☐	☐
4 Young people love to travel.	☐	☐
5 Fun activities are sometimes free.	☐	☐

2 🔊 Listen to the podcast again. Choose the word you hear.

1 *Doing / Watching* things makes people happier than buying things.
2 They love to be with their *friends / family*.
3 And it isn't always *expensive / free* to do things.
4 *These / Those* are the best things in life.
5 And they're *free / fun*!

LISTENING SKILL: Understanding numbers ▶2.3

3 🔊 Listen to the podcast again, and write the numbers you hear.

1 You spend _____ dollars on new sunglasses, and you're, oh, a little happy.

2 _____ % of young people like to spend money on doing things, not buying things.

3 My daughter is _____.

4 She's with her friends _____ days a week!

DISCUSSION BOARD PREPARATION

4 Look at the first sentence of the response. What question does it answer?

_____

Unit 2 Review Discussion Point

1   Read the quote. Is it true for you?
    "The moon belongs to everyone,
    The best things in life are free,
    The stars belong to everyone,
    They gleam there for you
    And me."
    —"The Best Things in Life Are Free" (1927 song), selected from the *Oxford Dictionary of Modern Quotations*, 3ʳᵈ ed., edited by Elizabeth Knowles
2   Are the best things in life free?
3   What are the best things in your life? Do they cost money or are they free?

Latest: Rich Guay
This quote isn't true for me. I don't think the best things in life are free. My favorite things are my new phone and my car. And I love to travel to beautiful places, eat at nice restaurants, and go to concerts with friends. These things aren't free. So, for me, the best things in life are expensive!

5 What are Rich's favorite things? Are they free?

6 Review the rubric. Use the rubric to give a score for the reply.
     Give points: 0 (not successful)–10 (successful).

Writing a Discussion Board Post	Points
The post answers the questions clearly and completely.	
The post uses singular and plural nouns, possessive adjectives, and demonstrative adjectives and pronouns correctly.	
The post shows careful thinking about the topic.	
Sentences are complete and have correct punctuation.	
The words are spelled correctly.	
The post is long enough (50–60 words).	
Total	

WRITE YOUR POST

7 Read the quote. Is it true for you? Are the best things in life free? What are the best things in your life? Do they cost money or are they free?

"The moon belongs to everyone,
The best things in life are free,
The stars belong to everyone,
They gleam there for you
And me."
—"The Best Things in Life Are Free" (1927 song), selected from the *Oxford Dictionary of Modern Quotations*, 3ʳᵈ ed., edited by Elizabeth Knowles

8 Use the rubric from Exercise 6 to score your post. Then improve your post.

 Go online to add your comments to the discussion board.

3 Places

There is... and *There are*... ▶3.1

1 Complete the sentences with *There is* or *There are*.

1 _____ a good café on South Street.

2 _____ many restaurants in Tokyo.

3 _____ one airport in my city.

4 _____ some beautiful parks in New York.

5 _____ five English teachers in our school.

6 _____ an interesting new museum on Webster Street.

2 Write sentences about the picture with *There is* and *There are*. Use singular or plural forms of the words in the box.

book	computer	pen
bag	key	phone

1 <u>There are four books on the table.</u>

2 _____

3 _____

4 _____

5 _____

6 _____

Imperatives ▶3.2

3 Match the beginning of the sentence in A with the ending in B.

A

1 Take a taxi ____

2 Try this ____

3 Go straight on ____

4 Don't visit here ____

5 Give me ____

6 Don't eat ____

B

a your phone number.

b at that restaurant.

c Forest Street.

d pizza. It's great!

e to your hotel.

f in the summer.

4 Complete the statements. Use positive or negative imperatives with the verbs in parentheses.

1 <u>Don't go</u> to that movie. It isn't good. (go)

2 _____ left on Park Street. Then go straight. (turn)

3 _____ at that hotel. It's very expensive. (stay)

4 _____ at that picture. It's beautiful! (look)

5 _____ that museum. It's very interesting. (visit)

There is / There are: *Yes/no* questions and negative statements ▶3.3

5 Complete the conversations with *Is there* or *Are there* and short answers.

1 A: _____ a train station in this town?

B: Yes, _____.

2 A: _____ any good restaurants near this hotel?

B: No, _____.

3 A: _____ a bathroom in this store?

B: No, _____.

4 A: _____ a bank on this street?

B: Yes, _____.

6 Complete the sentences with *There isn't a* or *There aren't any*.

1 _____ parks near here.

2 _____ café in this hotel.

3 _____ supermarket on my street.

4 _____ good movies at this theater tonight.

5 _____ dining room in my apartment.

Places in a town ▶3.1

1 What is in each place? Match.

___ 1	a café	a a chef
___ 2	an airport	b coffee
___ 3	a supermarket	c pictures
___ 4	a restaurant	d trees
___ 5	a park	e money
___ 6	a bank	f airplanes
___ 7	a museum	g fruit

2 Compete the sentences with places from Exercise 1.

1 I want some tea. Let's go to a _____.
2 The Pizza Palace is a great _____.
3 That's a beautiful _____. It's very green.
4 Heathrow is a very big _____.
5 Dalia likes math. She works in a _____.
6 The new science _____ is very interesting.
7 Food Land is my favorite _____ to shop at.

VOCABULARY DEVELOPMENT:
Prepositions of place ▶3.2

3 Complete the sentences with prepositions.

1 The circle is _____ the square.
2 The circle is _____ the square.
3 The circle is _____ the squares.
4 The circle is _____ the square.

4 Read the sentences. Choose the correct words.

1 There are nine rooms *in / on / near* the house.
2 The bank is *in / on / between* Main Street.
3 Our office building is *near / in / on* the airport.
4 The museum is *next to / in / between* a lake.
5 The beach is *in / on / next to* New Zealand.

5 Correct the mistakes in the **bold** phrases.

1 Our school is **in Center Street.** _____
2 There's a supermarket **near to my house.** _____
3 The museum is **next the park.** _____
4 The bank is **in the third floor.** _____
5 The café is **near of the bank** and the park. _____
6 Koji lives **on Japan.** _____

Rooms in a house ▶3.4

6 Unscramble the words to make rooms.

1 odrbemo _____
2 vligni mroo _____
3 eticnhk _____
4 lahl _____
5 gindni moro _____
6 hotrmboa _____

7 Where do you find each thing? Write rooms from Exercise 6.

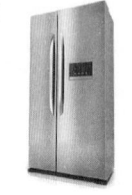 

1   2

_____ _____

3   4

_____ _____

8 Write the names of the rooms to complete the ad.

Come see this great apartment!

This apartment is perfect for students. There are two small but sunny ¹b_____, a beautiful new ²b_____, and a big ³k_____ and ⁴d_____ next to a large ⁵l_____.

1 Read the article. What place is it about? Where is the place?

New Orleans

Are you interested in music? Food? Architecture? Then visit New Orleans, Louisiana. It has architecture, music, and food from around the world—Irish, German, Spanish, and French.

The French Quarter is the oldest part of the city. Walk around the neighborhood, and look at the interesting buildings. Tour the Williams Residence. It's a beautiful old house on Royal Street.

New Orleans is a city of music. In the French Quarter, jazz musicians are everywhere. Learn about jazz (and hear a free concert) at the Jazz National Historic Park.

There are hundreds of restaurants in New Orleans. For terrific seafood, go to Antoine's. It's huge—there are 14 dining rooms! Have coffee and beignets (special donuts) at the French Quarter's famous Café du Monde.

—adapted from *The Oxford Encyclopedia of American Cultural and Intellectual History* edited by Joan Shelley Rubin and Scott E. Casper

2 Why is New Orleans a good place to visit? Which four reasons are in the article?

☐ It has architecture, music, and food from different countries.
☐ There are good beaches.
☐ There are beautiful buildings.
☐ You can listen to jazz music.
☐ It is quiet.
☐ There are many good restaurants.
☐ There are good hotels.
☐ It isn't expensive.

3 Choose *True* or *False*.

		True	False
1	The French Quarter is a new part of New Orleans.	☐	☐
2	New Orleans is in Florida.	☐	☐
3	The author of the article likes New Orleans.	☐	☐
4	The Williams Residence is an ugly house.	☐	☐
5	There are many jazz musicians in the French Quarter.	☐	☐
6	Concerts at the Jazz National Historic Park are expensive.	☐	☐
7	Antoine's is a very big restaurant.	☐	☐
8	You can have coffee at the Café du Monde.	☐	☐

READING SKILL: Identifying and understanding proper nouns ▶3.1

4 Answer the questions.

1 How can you identify a proper noun?
   a It has *a* or *an* in front of it.
   b It begins with a capital letter.
   c It has *the* in front of it.

2 Which of these is *not* a proper noun?
   a names of cities
   b names of countries
   c words for family
   d people's names
   e languages

5 Read the article again. Write each proper noun in the article next to the correct common noun.

1 a restaurant _____

2 a café _____

3 a city _____

4 a state _____

5 a neighborhood _____

6 a park _____

7 a street _____

8 a house _____

6 Look at the reading on page 3 of this workbook. Find the proper nouns. Complete the chart with proper nouns and common nouns.

Common noun	Proper noun(s)
	Petr
woman's name	
	1 Prague 2 3
countries	1 2
	1 Czech 2 3

REAL-WORLD ENGLISH: Giving directions ▶3.4

1 Complete the dialogue from the video with words from the box.

go	left	take	turn	use	walk

Woman: Oh, wow. I'm really lost.

Max: Oh, that's OK. Uh…so here's Seventh Street. ¹_____ straight. ²_____
a few blocks, and ³_____ left on Main Street. There's a shop on the corner.

Woman: OK. So…Seventh, and then ⁴_____ on Main.

Max: Right. So, walk on Main Street until you see High Street and ⁵_____ a right.
The Commons is the big red building on the corner of Wells Avenue. There are
two entrances. ⁶_____ the left entrance for Rowan Hall.

Woman: OK. Got it. Thank you so much!

2 Look at the map. Speaker A is at the Hotel Bondi.
Complete the conversations.

1 A: How do I get to the Pacific Shopping Mall?

B: _____

2 A: Excuse me. Where's the Bondi Market?

B: _____

3 A: How do I get to the ANZ Bank?

B: _____

4 A: Excuse me. Where is Bondi Beach?

B: _____

3 Are these imperatives rude or not rude?

	Rude	Not rude
1 Take the bus to Beach Road.	☐	☐
2 Try Harry's Café. They have great coffee.	☐	☐
3 Go home now.	☐	☐
4 Push that button.	☐	☐
5 Go to Bondi Beach. It's beautiful!	☐	☐
6 Cook dinner.	☐	☐
7 Don't visit the art museum. It's very small.	☐	☐
8 Give me some water.	☐	☐

UNIT REVIEW: Podcast

Go online and listen to the podcast from the Unit Review.

1 Listen to the podcast. Who says each sentence—Speaker 1, 2, or 3?

	Speaker 1	Speaker 2	Speaker 3
1 It's in a fun neighborhood.	☐	☐	☐
2 It's big and sunny.	☐	☐	☐
3 That's home sweet home!	☐	☐	☐
4 There isn't a lot to clean.	☐	☐	☐
5 That's my perfect home.	☐	☐	☐

2 Listen to the podcast again. Complete the sentences.

1 It's a _____ house.

2 It's near a _____ park.

3 It's on the top floor of a tall _____ building.

4 It's _____ the beach.

5 There are a lot of _____, stores, and _____ near it.

6 It's an apartment in an _____ building.

LISTENING SKILL: Understanding why you are listening: Specific information ▶3.3

3 Listen to the podcast again. What rooms are in each person's perfect home? Take notes in the chart.

Speaker	Rooms
1	5 bedrooms
2	
3	

DISCUSSION BOARD PREPARATION

4 Look at the Unit 3 Discussion Point. Read the questions in the prompt. Then read the reply. Is the quote true for the writer?

_____

Unit 3 Review Discussion Point

1   Read the quote. What does it mean?
    "Home, sweet home."
    —title of song from "Clari, or, The Maid of Milan" (1823 opera), selected from *Oxford Essential Quotations*, 5ᵗʰ ed., edited by Susan Ratcliffe
2   Is it true for you?
3   What makes a home "sweet" for you?

Latest: **Catherine**
This quote means that home is a great place. This is true for me. My home is my favorite place. Mostly, it's because my family is there. Also, it's sunny and comfortable. It's in a nice, quiet neighborhood. There's a beautiful park near my apartment, and I walk there every day. For me, a "sweet" home is a happy home.

---

5   What is the writer's favorite place? What does she like about the place?

6   Review the rubric. Use the rubric to give a score for the reply.
Give points: 0 (not successful)–10 (successful).

Writing a Discussion Board Post	Points
The post answers the questions clearly and completely.	
Sentences have subject-verb agreement.	
The post uses *There is / There are* correctly.	
The post shows careful thinking about the topic.	
Sentences are complete and have correct punctuation.	
The post is long enough (50–60 words).	
Total	

WRITE YOUR POST

7   Read the quote. What does it mean? Is it true for you? What makes a home "sweet" for you?

"Home, sweet home."
—title of song from "Clari, or, The Maid of Milan" (1823 opera), selected from *Oxford Essential Quotations*, 5ᵗʰ ed., edited by Susan Ratcliffe

8   Use the rubric from Exercise 6 to score your post. Then improve your post.

 Go online to add your comments to the discussion board.

4 Life

Simple present ▶4.1

1 Read the paragraph. Find the verbs in the simple present.

My name (is) Carson. I (live) with my two brothers, Curtis and Connor. We have a small apartment in the city. I am a college student. Curtis works at a café, and Connor has a job at an art museum. In the evenings, I do homework, and my brothers watch TV. On weekends, we go to the beach.

2 Choose the correct form of the verb to complete the sentence.

1 I *like / likes* this book.
2 You *study / studies* a lot!
3 He *live / lives* near me.
4 They *have / has* a big family.
5 She *miss / misses* her family.
6 They *love / loves* music.
7 I *have / has* one sister.
8 We *want / wants* pizza for dinner.
9 He *have / has* brown hair.
10 I *go / goes* to bed late.

3 Complete the sentences with the simple present of the verbs in parentheses.

My name is Mia. I'm an author. I ¹_____ (write) children's books. My husband, Tom, ²_____ (work) at a bank. We ³_____ (like) our jobs. We ⁴_____ (have) two children. Our daughter, Hannah, is twelve. Our son, Finn, is ten. They ⁵_____ (go) to school at 8:00 in the morning, and they ⁶_____ (come) home at 3:00. After school, Hannah ⁷_____ (play) soccer, and Finn plays tennis. We ⁸_____ (live) on a quiet street in a small town.

Simple present: *Yes/no* questions ▶4.2

4 Complete the questions about the family in Exercise 3. Use *do* or *does*. Write short answers.

1 A: _____ Tom work at a restaurant?
  B: _____

2 A: _____ Mia write books?
  B: _____

3 A: _____ they like their jobs?
  B: _____

4 A: _____ Mia and Tom have three children?
  B: _____

5 A: _____ Hannah play tennis after school?
  B: _____

5 Change the sentences to *yes/no* questions.

1 She works at a hotel. *Does she work at a hotel?*
2 You go to work early. _____
3 They work on weekends. _____
4 Shannon loves music. _____
5 Kwan lives near his school. _____

Simple present: Negative forms ▶4.3

6 Choose *don't* or *doesn't* to complete the sentences.

1 I *don't / doesn't* get up early.
2 She *don't / doesn't* have a brother.
3 You *don't / doesn't* have a lot of free time.
4 They *don't / doesn't* watch a lot of TV.
5 We *don't / doesn't* work at night.

7 Make the sentences about the brothers in Exercise 1 negative. Then correct the sentences.

1 Curtis works at an airport.
  Curtis doesn't work at an airport. He works at a café.

2 Connor has a job at a science museum.
  _____

3 The brothers live in a big apartment.
  _____

4 Carson watches TV in the evenings.
  _____

5 They go to the beach on Wednesdays.
  _____

Family ▶4.1

1 Write the family words in the correct column.

brother	father	mother	son
daughter	husband	sister	wife

Female	Male
	brother

2 Look at the picture. Complete the sentences with words from Exercise 1.

Eva
Marc
Sylvia
Sam

1 Eva is Sylvia and Sam's _____.

2 Sam is Eva and Marc's _____.

3 Marc is Sam's _____.

4 Eva is Marc's _____.

5 Sam is Sylvia's _____.

6 Marc is Eva's _____.

7 Sylvia is Eva and Marc's _____.

8 Sylvia is Sam's _____.

3 Match the beginning of the sentence in A with the ending in B.

A	B
___ 1 My mother's son is	a my brother.
___ 2 My daughter's brother is	b my sister.
___ 3 My brother's father is	c my son.
___ 4 My father's wife is	d my daughter.
___ 5 My son's sister is	e my mother.
___ 6 My father's daughter is	f my father.

Habit/routine verbs ▶4.2

4 Unscramble the letters to make verb phrases.

1 peles tale   s_____ l_____

2 og ot het ymg g_____ _____
                 _____ _____

3 vhae krbafetsa h_____ b_____

4 od mewhroko   d_____ h_____

5 tge edray   g_____ _____

5 Complete the sentences with a phrase from Exercise 4.

1 I _____ for work at 7:30 in the morning.

2 I _____ at a café. I have eggs and coffee.

3 I _____ in the afternoon. I exercise for one hour.

4 I _____ for my math class in the evening.

5 I _____ on Saturdays. I get up at 11:00 or 12:00!

VOCABULARY DEVELOPMENT:
Prepositions of time: *On*, *in*, and *at* ▶4.3

6 Match the times and days in A with the words in B.

A		B	
___ 1	9:00 a.m.	a	night
___ 2	2:00 p.m.	b	morning
___ 3	7:00 p.m.	c	evening
___ 4	11:00 p.m.	d	weekend
___ 5	Saturday and Sunday	e	afternoon

7 Read the sentences. Choose the correct words.

1 I do homework in *the afternoon / afternoon*.

2 Eli goes to the gym on *Mondays / the evening*.

3 We don't work on *night / weekends*.

4 I exercise in *the morning / the night*.

5 Jen spends time with her friends at *the morning / night*.

6 My family has a big dinner on *New Year's Day / the night*.

8 Complete the sentences with *on*, *in*, or *at*.

1 I study _____ the evening.

2 Kwan has English class _____ Tuesdays.

3 We get up early _____ the morning.

4 I have breakfast _____ 8:00.

5 They play video games _____ the afternoon.

6 Sandra starts work _____ 2:00.

READING: Practice

1 Read the article. Does Mark Zuckerberg live like a typical billionaire?

A "Typical" Billionaire

In 2006, Mark Zuckerberg started Facebook with three classmates at Harvard University. Now he is one of the richest people in the world! But he doesn't live like a rich person. He has a pretty typical routine: He gets up at 8:00. Then he checks Facebook on his phone. Next, he usually exercises. Then he gets ready for work. Every day, he wears jeans, a gray T-shirt, and sneakers. After that, he has breakfast.

Zuckerberg works about 50–60 hours a week. In the evening, he usually spends time with his wife and two young daughters. He sings to his daughters before bed. He also likes to learn new things. He is learning Mandarin Chinese. And he reads two books every month. He also has another job: He started Internet.org. It is trying to bring Internet access to everyone in the world. Zuckerberg is a very busy man!

—adapted from *A Dictionary of Computer Science* edited by Andrew Butterfield and Gerard Ekembe Ngondi

2 What does Mark Zuckerberg do every day? Order his activities (1–7).

_____ checks Facebook

_____ sings to his daughters

_____ has breakfast

_____ spends time with his family

_____ exercises

_____ gets up

_____ gets ready for work

3 Choose *True* or *False*.

	True	False
1 Three people started Facebook.	☐	☐
2 Mark Zuckerberg looks at his phone in the morning.	☐	☐
3 He wears many different clothes.	☐	☐
4 He works a lot.	☐	☐
5 He has two children.	☐	☐
6 He is learning a new language.	☐	☐
7 He reads about thirty books every year.	☐	☐
8 He has a lot of free time.	☐	☐

READING SKILL: Identifying key words: Nouns, verbs, adjectives ▶4.2

4 Read these sentences from the article. Choose all the key words. (Remember: Key words are nouns, verbs, and adjectives.)

1 He has a pretty (typical) (routine.)
2 Then he checks Facebook on his phone.
3 Every day, he wears jeans, a gray T-shirt, and sneakers.
4 Zuckerberg works about 50–60 hours a week.
5 He likes to learn new things.
6 Mark Zuckerberg spends time with his family in the evening.
7 It is trying to bring Internet access to everyone in the world.
8 He is a very busy man!

5 Put the key words from Exercise 4 in the correct category in the chart.

Nouns	Verbs	Adjectives
routine		typical

6 Look at the reading on page 24 of this workbook. Find more key words, and add them to the chart above.

7 Look at the reading on page 17 of this workbook. Find key words, and write them in the correct category in the chart.

Nouns	Verbs	Adjectives

REAL-WORLD ENGLISH: Asking for the time ▶4.4

1 Complete the dialogue from the video with words from the box.

10:25	half	it's	the time	late	what time

Andy: Ugh! Where is it? I'm ¹_____!

Max: Late? You're not late. ²_____ ten past ten.

Andy: Uh, yes, I am!

Max: Wait…How is that possible? ³_____ is it?

Andy: The power is out. The clock is wrong. I don't know what

time it is. ⁴_____ maybe?

Max: There's no power…?

Andy: Uh…do you have your phone?

Max: Yes, but I always turn it off and put it in my rucksack before class…Just a second…

Andy: OK…What's ⁵_____?

Max: It's ⁶_____ past. 10:30. Time to go!

2 Write the time in words. Write each time two ways.

1 3:15 _____three fifteen_____ _____quarter past three_____

2 11:05 _____ _____

3 6:30 _____ _____

4 8:45 _____ _____

5 2:00 _____ _____

6 12:20 _____ _____

3 Write the words in the correct order to make questions about the time.

1 the / hey / time / what's

_____

2 me / the / you / do / have / excuse / time

_____

3 it / time / what / is

_____

4 me / you / know / excuse / do / time / it / what / is

_____

4 Look at the questions in Exercise 3. Is the person talking to a friend (F) or a stranger (S)?

Question 1 ____

Question 2 ____

Question 3 ____

Question 4 ____

UNIT REVIEW: Podcast

Go online and listen to the podcast from the Unit Review.

1 🔊 Listen to the podcast. Which activity isn't mentioned?

a   Get up early every day.

b   Go to the theater.

c   Spend time with friends.

d   Do the same things every day.

e   Go to the gym.

2 🔊 Look at the activities below. Then listen to the podcast again. Who does each activity? Write *J* (Jake) or *A* (Alexa).

1   gets up at 7:00   _____

2   goes to work at 8:30   _____

3   goes to the gym   _____

4   goes home at 6:00   _____

5   watches TV in the evening   _____

6   takes an art class   _____

7   goes to bed at 11:00   _____

8   walks on the beach on Fridays   _____

LISTENING SKILL: Contractions (short forms) with *be* and simple present negatives ▶4.3

3 🔊 Listen to the podcast again. Choose the correct word.

1   Jake *has / doesn't have* the same routine every day.

2   Jake's life *is / isn't very* interesting.

3   Alexa *has / doesn't have* the same routine every day.

4   On Mondays and Wednesdays, she *gets up / doesn't get up* early.

5   On Tuesday and Thursday mornings, she *exercises / doesn't exercise*.

6   Alexa's life *is / isn't* interesting.

DISCUSSION BOARD PREPARATION

4   Look at the Unit 4 Discussion Point. Read the questions in the prompt. Then read the reply. Is the quote true for the writer?

_____

Unit 4 Review Discussion Point

1 Read the quote. Is it true for you?
   "The less of routine, the more of life."
   —Amos Bronson Alcott, selected from *Oxford Essential Quotations,* 5th ed., edited by Susan Ratcliffe
2 Is your daily routine busy? Do you have time to do fun things?
3 Do you like to have the same routine every day? Why or why not?

Latest: **Marissa**
This quote means that it is not good to do the same things every day. This is not true for me. I like to have the same routine every day. It's comfortable and relaxing, and not too busy. I like to get up at the same time, eat the same thing for breakfast, and go to work at the same time. I like to spend time with the same friends in the evenings. I don't have to think about the little things, so I can think about the big things!

5 Does the writer like her daily routine? Why or why not?

6 Review the rubric. Use the rubric to give a score for the reply.
Give points: 0 (not successful)–10 (successful).

Writing a Discussion Board Post	Points
The post answers the questions clearly and completely.	
Sentences have subject-verb agreement.	
The post uses the simple present correctly.	
The post shows careful thinking about the topic.	
Sentences are complete and have correct punctuation.	
The post is long enough (50–60 words).	
Total	

WRITE YOUR POST

7 Read the quote. Is your daily routine busy? Do you have time to do fun things? Do you like to have the same routine every day? Why or why not?

"The less of routine, the more of life."
—Amos Bronson Alcott, selected from *Oxford Essential Quotations,* 5th ed., edited by Susan Ratcliffe

8 Use the rubric from Exercise 6 to score your post. Then improve your post.

 Go online to add your comments to the discussion board.

5 Travel

GRAMMAR

Adverbs of frequency ▶5.1

1 Write the adverb of frequency in the correct place in each sentence.

1 I ___usually___ take _____ the bus to work. (usually)

2 The bus _____ isn't _____ late. (often)

3 Riley _____ visits _____ her parents on weekends. (sometimes)

4 Her parents _____ are _____ happy to see her. (always)

5 They _____ go _____ to restaurants together. (sometimes)

6 We don't _____ go on _____ vacation in July. (always)

7 Our vacation _____ is _____ fun. (usually)

8 We _____ visit _____ museums on vacation. (never)

2 Read the chart about Nick's week. Complete the sentences with adverbs of frequency.

	Mon.	Tues.	Wed.	Thurs.	Fri.
walks to work	✓				
drives to work		✓	✓	✓	✓
bikes to work					
runs after work		✓		✓	✓
has lunch at his desk	✓	✓	✓	✓	

1 Nick _____ walks to work.

2 He _____ drives to work.

3 He _____ bikes to work.

4 He _____ runs after work.

5 He _____ has lunch at his desk.

Like / love / hate + a verb in the -ing form ▶5.2

3 Complete the sentences with the correct form of a verb from the box.

eat	go	fly	learn	travel	work

1 Mei loves _____ languages.

2 Katie hates _____. She always travels by train.

3 Peter doesn't like _____. He loves weekends.

4 They like _____ at restaurants.

5 I love _____. I'm going to Thailand next summer.

4 Read the sentence. Write another sentence with love / like / don't like / hate + -ing.

1 Mina never goes to the stores in town. (shop)
   Mina hates shopping.

2 Hector's job isn't intereseting. (go to work)
   _____

3 We always take our bikes with us on vacation. (bike)
   _____

4 I often eat pizza for lunch. (eat pizza)
   _____

5 Anne doesn't usually drink tea. (drink tea)
   _____

The present simple: Wh- questions ▶5.3

5 Choose do or does to complete the questions.

1 Where do / does you live?
2 How do / does he get to class?
3 When do / does they exercise?
4 What do / does she usually have for breakfast?
5 Why do / does they ride their bikes everywhere?

6 Complete the questions.

1 A: Where _____?
   B: He usually stays at an Airbnb.

2 A: What _____?
   B: They usually have fish and vegetables for dinner.

3 A: Why _____?
   B: She walks to work because it's near her house.

4 A: How _____?
   B: I get to work by bus.

Unit 5 Travel

29

Transportation ▶5.1

1 Choose the correct word to complete each sentence.

1 Celia lives a mile from work. She goes to work by ____.

   a plane   b boat   c car

2 I live in New York. Every summer, I visit my friends in Hong Kong. I travel by ____.

   a car   b subway   c plane

3 Toshio has a new ____.

   a subway   b train   c motorcycle

4 There is a ____ stop near my house.

   a car   b bus   c bike

5 My brother gets seasick, so he doesn't travel by ____.

   a boat   b car   c plane

6 I like to travel by ____ because there isn't any traffic.

   a subway   b bus   c car

2 Complete the sentences with a word from the box.

bike	boat	car	plane	subway

1 I hate flying. I don't like traveling by _____.

2 He never drives. He doesn't have a _____.

3 We can take the _____ from this station into the center of the city.

4 Do you like sailing? We have a _____. Meet us at the beach tomorrow!

5 Riding a _____ on the street in the city is dangerous.

Travel verbs ▶5.2

3 Unscramble the words to make travel verbs.

1 vredi _____   5 lkaw _____

2 kieb _____   6 lfy _____

3 kaet _____   7 erdi _____

4 sila _____

4 Complete the sentences with words from Exercise 3.

1 We usually _____ from Narita Airport in Tokyo.

2 He can't _____ a car. He's only 15.

3 Amelia doesn't _____ to work in the winter because there is snow on the roads.

4 In the summer, we _____ our boat in the ocean.

5 I _____ to work on nice days.

6 They _____ the subway to work. It's fast and cheap.

VOCABULARY DEVELOPMENT: Agent nouns: Verb + -er and noun + -ist ▶5.3

5 Are the words nouns (N) or verbs (V)?

1 science ____

2 write ____

3 drive ____

4 art ____

5 guitar ____

6 travel ____

6 Circle the correct word to complete each sentence.

1 This class is long. I need to _____ a break.

   a make   b take   c do

2 When I'm tired, I often _____ a mistake.

   a make   b take   c do

3 Sarah wants to _____ well at her job.

   a make   b take   c do

4 We study hard before we _____ a test.

   a make   b take   c do

5 Do you want to _____ homework together?

   a make   b take   c do

6 My classmates _____ really helpful notes.

   a make   b take   c do

7 Write a word under each picture. Use *-ist* or *-er* forms of the words in Exercise 5.

1

_____

2

_____

3

_____

4

_____

5

_____

6

_____

8 Write the words from Exercise 7 in the correct category. Then think of more *-ist* and *-er* words and write them in the chart.

-ist words	*-er* words

READING SKILL: Using headings ▶5.3

1 Before you read the article, look at the headings. What questions do you think the article answers?

☐ What does *road rage* mean?
☐ What do people with road rage do?
☐ How many people have road rage?
☐ In what countries is road rage a big problem?
☐ How can we stop road rage?

2 What can you learn in each section? Complete the chart.

What can I learn?	Section (1, 2, or 3)
How can I *not* have road rage?	
The definition of *road rage*	
Do I have road rage?	

3 Read the article. What does *rage* mean?

QR Road Rage

Road rage makes our roads dangerous. We need to stop it!

1 What is road rage?

Drivers sometimes get very angry. They have road rage. Road rage is the reason for 20–30% of car accidents.

2 Do you have road rage?

Do you do these things? Then maybe you have road rage.

1 You see a red light, and you drive faster.

2 The car in front of you is driving slowly. You drive very close to the other car.

3 You're sitting at a red light. The light turns green. The car in front of you doesn't go. You honk your car's horn loudly.

3 Stopping road rage

To stop road rage, relax! Try these things:

1 Listen to quiet music or an audio book.

2 Sleep a lot at night.

3 Exercise often.

4 Leave ten minutes early.

—adapted from *A Dictionary of Public Health* edited by John Last

READING: Practice

4 Choose *True* or *False*.

	True	False
1 *Road rage* means driving when you are angry.	☐	☐
2 Road rage is not a big problem.	☐	☐
3 People with road rage stop quickly for a red light.	☐	☐
4 Some drivers get angry because other cars drive slowly.	☐	☐
5 People with road rage are loud.	☐	☐
6 You can't stop road rage.	☐	☐

5 How can you stop road rage? Choose the correct answers.

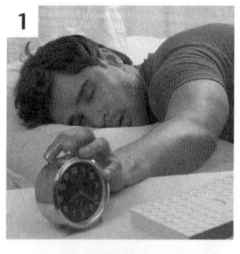

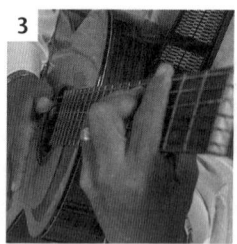

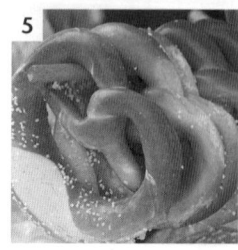

_____ 1 Leave ten minutes early.

_____ 2 Drive a cool car.

_____ 3 Listen to quiet music.

_____ 4 Talk on your phone in the car.

_____ 5 Eat food in the car.

_____ 6 Wear sunglasses.

_____ 7 Sleep a lot at night.

_____ 8 Exercise often.

REAL-WORLD ENGLISH: Asking someone to repeat something ▶5.4

1 Complete the dialogue from the video with words from the box.

huh	I said	sorry

Andy: My mom loves cooking for guests.

Max: ¹_____? What?

Andy: ²_____, my mom loves cooking. Her food is amazing.

Max: Oh! Good!

Andy: What's that?

Max: ³_____?

Andy: What is that?

2 Complete the dialogue from the video with words from the box.

have them	he said	repeat that	sorry	what

Max: Hey, do you have the tickets?

Andy: He said we need to go to track 5.

Max: ¹_____?

Andy: Track 5.

Max: No, no no. I asked if you have the tickets.

....

Attendant: There's a track change. Go to track six for train 64.

Andy: ²_____, could you ³_____?

Attendant: Sure…Train 64 now leaves from gate six.

3 Look at the numbered expressions in the dialogues above. What does each expression do?

____ 1   a   repeats only the most important information

____ 2   b   asks a friend to repeat something

____ 3   c   asks a person they don't know well to repeat something

____ 4   d   repeats in different words

4 Complete the conversations. Follow the instructions in brackets.

1   Your friend: Hey, bad news, our bus is late.

    Your friend: Sorry?

    You: _____ [Repeat only the most important information.]

2   Bus station attendant: The bus leaves at 3:30 from gate 17.

    You: _____ [Ask the person to repeat specific information.]

    Bus station attendant: 3:30.

3   Your friend: Our bus is here.

    You: _____ [Ask a friend to repeat.]

    Your friend: That's our bus. It's here.

UNIT REVIEW: Podcast

Go online and listen to the podcast from the Unit Review.

1 Listen to the podcast. Choose *True* or *False*.

		True	False
1	Many people like traveling with family and friends.	☐	☐
2	Sofia likes traveling with family and friends.	☐	☐
3	Sofia's friends are angry at her.	☐	☐
4	Sofia likes reading.	☐	☐
5	Sofia never travels by car.	☐	☐
6	Sofia doesn't like going to museums.	☐	☐

2 Listen to the podcast again. What are some good things about traveling alone? Choose the things that Sofia talks about.

1 You meet new people. ☐
2 You sleep a lot. ☐
3 You don't spend a lot of money. ☐
4 You read a lot of books. ☐
5 You listen to your favorite music. ☐
6 You choose the restaurants. ☐
7 You take a lot of photos. ☐
8 You go where you want to go. ☐

LISTENING SKILL: Listening for Specific Information ▶5.1

3 Read the sentences below. Then listen to the podcast again. Complete the sentences with adverbs of frequency from the box.

always	never	often	sometimes	usually

1 Friends _____ ask me that.
2 I _____ meet interesting people.
3 I _____ talk to other travelers.
4 I _____ make new friends.
5 I _____ go to museums.

DISCUSSION BOARD PREPARATION

4 Look at the Unit 5 Discussion Point. Read the questions in the prompt. Then read the reply. Is the quote true for the writer?

_____

Unit 5 Review Discussion Point

1   Read the quote. Do you usually travel with friends, with family, or by yourself?
    "It is easier to find a travelling companion than to get rid of one."
    —Peg Bracken, selected from *The Oxford Dictionary of Humorous Quotations*, 5th ed., edited by
    Gyles Brandreth
2   Do you like traveling alone? Why or why not?

Latest: **Emir**
I usually travel with my friends. It's really fun. We always talk a lot and laugh a lot! It's also cheaper because we share travel expenses, like gas and Uber fares. We also share a hotel room or house. Also, I don't like going places and eating in restaurants alone. I like having dinner with friends.

5   Who does the writer like to travel with? Why?

6   Review the rubric. Use the rubric to give a score for the reply.
    Give points: 0 (not successful)–10 (successful).

Writing a Discussion Board Post	Points
The post answers the questions clearly and completely.	
The post uses adverbs of frequency correctly.	
The post uses *like / love / hate* + a verb in the *-ing* form correctly.	
The post shows careful thinking about the topic.	
Sentences are complete and have correct punctuation.	
The post is long enough (50–60 words).	
Total	

WRITE YOUR POST

7   Read the quote. Do you usually travel with friends, with family, or by yourself? Do you like traveling alone? Why or why not?

"It is easier to find a travelling companion than to get rid of one."
—Peg Bracken, selected from *The Oxford Dictionary of Humorous Quotations*, 5th ed., edited by Gyles Brandreth

8   Use the rubric from Exercise 6 to score your post. Then improve your post.

 Go online to add your comments to the discussion board.

6 Skills

Can / can't for ability ▶6.1

1 Correct the mistakes in the **bold** phrases.

1 He **cans run** fast. _____

2 I **can't to drive** a car. _____

3 She **can paints** well. _____

4 They **do can play** the guitar. _____

5 She **can't not speak** Korean. _____

2 Read the chart about what people can and can't do. Write sentences with *can* or *can't* and a verb.

	play tennis	speak French	drive a car	swim 5k
me	✓	✗	✓	✓
you	✓	✓	✗	✗
we	✓	✓	✗	✗
Rita	✗	✓	✗	✓
Aiden and Jack	✗	✓	✓	✗

1 I _____ _____ French.

2 Aiden and Jack _____ _____ tennis.

3 You _____ _____ five kilometers!

4 Rita _____ _____ a car.

5 We _____ _____ French.

6 Aiden and Jack _____ _____ a car.

7 I _____ _____ tennis.

8 Rita _____ _____ five kilometers.

Adverbs of manner ▶6.2

3 Read the sentences. Is the **bold** word an adjective or an adverb?

		Adverb	Adjective
1	I do my homework **carefully**.	☐	☐
2	That car is very **fast**!	☐	☐
3	They run **fast**.	☐	☐
4	You play the guitar **well**.	☐	☐
5	That's a **fun** computer game.	☐	☐

4 Complete the sentences with the adverb form of each adjective.

1 Luis Suárez plays soccer very _____. (good)

2 You sing _____. (beautiful)

3 Michael Phelps can very swim _____. (fast)

4 Helen plays the guitar _____. (bad)

5 Beth Rodden can climb mountains _____. (quick)

Yes/no questions with can ▶6.3

5 Write the words in the correct order to make questions.

1 David / can / basketball / play

_____?

2 can / photos / beautiful / take / you

_____?

3 the guitar / they / play / can

_____?

4 high / jump / can / Ichika

_____?

5 you / Russian / speak / can

_____?

6 Write *yes/no* questions and short answers with *can* about the people in Exercise 2.

1 Aiden and Jack / speak French

A: _Can Aiden and Jack speak French?_

B: _Yes, they can._

2 Rita / drive a car

A: _____

B: _____

3 you / speak French

A: _____

B: _____

4 Rita / swim five kilometers

A: _____

B: _____

5 Aiden and Jack / play tennis

A: _____

B: _____

Abilities (verbs) ▶6.1

1 Match the beginning of the sentence in A with the ending in B.

A		B	
1	You draw ____	a	mountains.
2	I can't remember ____	b	his name.
3	Yunseo can speak ____	c	almost a meter!
4	We love climbing ____	d	beautiful pictures.
5	I can't see ____	e	three languages
6	He can jump ____	f	the board. I need my glasses.

2 Use the verbs in the box to complete the sentences.

climb	jump	remember	speaks	paint	see

1 Lila _____ English at work every day.

2 They want to _____ their kitchen blue.

3 Spider Man can _____ high.

4 I can't _____ my phone number!

5 We _____ mountains in the summer.

Sports and activities ▶6.2

3 Unscramble the words.

1	nisten	t_____	4	lbasbektla	b_____
2	emctruop	c_____	5	taguri	g_____
3	nsog	s_____	6	opthos	p_____

4 Choose the correct word from Exercise 3 to complete each sentence.

1 Adam plays _____ well because he's very tall.

2 My roommate plays the _____ very loudly.

3 You need exercise. Stop playing _____ games!

4 Katie can take _____ with her new phone.

5 My husband usually sings a _____ to our baby before bed.

6 Serena Williams is a great _____ player.

VOCABULARY DEVELOPMENT:
Adjective + *at* + noun ▶6.3

5 What is each person good at? Write sentences.

basketball	languages	painting
cooking	math	playing the guitar

1 Cynthia can jump high.

   She's good at basketball.

2 Paul remembers new words easily.

   _____

3 My aunt is an artist.

   _____

4 Maria loves having friends to her house for dinner.

   _____

5 Ahmed likes working with numbers.

   _____

6 Lydia is a musician.

   _____

6 Correct the mistakes in the **bold** phrases.

1 They **is terrible at playing** tennis. _____

2 She **is great with singing**. _____

3 He **is good at play** computer games. _____

4 They **are great at to taking** photos. _____

5 I **am bad at to paint**. _____

7 Complete each sentence with the *-ing* form of a word from the box.

climb mountains	play tennis	write
play soccer	sing	

1 JK Rowling is great at _____.

2 Beth Rodden is good at _____.

3 Venus and Serena Williams are great at _____.

4 Bruno Mars is good at _____.

5 Cristiano Ronaldo is great at _____.

REAL-WORLD READING

1 Read the article. What is multitasking?

Multitasking—Good or Bad?

Can you text your friends and listen to music and play a computer game—at the same time? You probably can. These days, people multitask all the time. We never do only one thing.

Is multitasking a good thing? The answer isn't simple. Multitasking can help you be successful at work. You can go to a meeting, answer emails, and write a report at the same time.

But most people aren't good at multitasking: 98% of people don't multitask well. Some companies know this, so they have rules for meetings: laptops closed and no checking cell phones. They want people to focus on the discussion.

Do you love multitasking? Then be a nurse, a teacher, a chef, or a businessperson. If you don't like multitasking, be an artist, an author, or a scientist.

—adapted from *A Dictionary of Human Resource Management*, 3rd ed., by Edmund Heery and Mike Noon

2 Read the article again. Answer the questions.

1 When do people multitask?
   a only on weekends   b always   c only at work

2 What can multitasking help you do?
   a work   b be happy   c listen to music

3 How many people are good at multitasking?
   a 2%   b 98%   c nobody

4 Why do companies have rules about multitasking at meetings?
   a so people aren't late   b so people can multitask
   c so people listen to the conversation

5 Does everyone like multitasking?
   a yes   b no   c The article doesn't say.

3 Choose the word that is different. Use the information in the article to explain why.

1 go to a meeting   answer emails   ⟨watch a movie⟩
   The others are both _work activities_.

2 listen to music   write a report   text your friends
   The others are both _____.

3 Don't open your laptop.   Don't look at your phone.   Don't talk.
   The others are both _____.

4 artist   author   chef
   The others are both _____.

5 nurse   teacher   scientist
   The others are both _____.

READING SKILL: Taking notes with important words ▶6.1

4 Look at the two papers with student notes about the article on page 24 of this workbook. Which notes are better? Why?

Student 1's notes

Mark Zuckerberg

He started Facebook with classmates at Harvard.

He has a typical routine.

He gets up at 8.

He checks Facebook.

He exercises.

He wears the same clothes every day.

Student 2's notes

Zuckerberg

2006 – started FB – 3 classmates

5th richest person/world

routine – typical

8 – gets up

clothes – same every day

work – 50–60 hrs/wk

family – evenings – sings

learning – Mandarin, 2 books/month

5 Read the article about multitasking again. Complete the notes.

Multitasking

= doing more than ^{1}_____ thing

multitasking—important at ^{2}_____

good? answer not ^{3}_____

^{4}_____% don't do it well

rules for meetings—closed ^{5}_____, no ^{6}_____

+ multitasking ⟶ teacher, ^{7}_____, ^{8}_____, ^{9}_____

– multitasking ⟶ artist, ^{10}_____, ^{11}_____

REAL-WORLD ENGLISH: Keeping the conversation going ▶6.4

1 Read the dialogues from the video. Choose the correct words.

Max: Uh, everything's fine, thanks.

Kevin: ¹*So / Then*, you're an artist, right?

Max: Yes. Uh...well, art is my major. ²*How about you? / What are you?*

Kevin: I don't know. Right now, I have a lot of science and technology classes.

....

Kevin: Hey. That's good! I can't paint or draw, so...

Max: **Oh, really? Not at all?**

Kevin: Nah, I don't like art very much. Oh, I mean...I don't like making art...or, like going to museums and stuff. But your art is great!

Max: Right. Right. Thanks.

Kevin: ³*What about you? / What do you do?* You must love going to museums.

Max: Uh, well, yes, actually, I do.

Kevin: **This place is great,** ⁴*OK / right?*

Max: Yeah. Yeah. I, um...I can watch football...um, soccer, uh, every Saturday at 11 a.m.!

Kevin: Right. Yeah, I don't really like...Sorry, I mean, I can't play soccer very well, so...

Max: I see.

Kevin: I'm terrible at kicking! But Andy...Andy can play soccer very well. He's great at it!

Max: Oh. ⁵*What of / What about* **American football?**

Kevin: I love watching American football but I can't play. **I play tennis. What about you?**

2 Look at the phrases in **bold** in the dialogues above. Which strategy does each phrase use to keep the conversation going? Write the phrase next to the correct strategy in the chart.

Strategy	Phrase(s)
asks about the other person after giving information about himself	
responds with interest and asks for more details	
looks for something in common	
changes the subject and asks a new question	

3 Read the conversations. Use each strategy to add to the conversations to keep them going.

1 A: Do you like basketball?

    B: No, not really. _____

    [Strategy: Change the subject and ask a new question]

2 A: This is great music, isn't it?

    B: Actually, I don't like jazz music. _____

    [Strategy: Look for something in common]

3 A: I'm a chef.

    B: _____

    [Strategy: Respond with interest and ask for more details]

4 A: I love science fiction books. _____

    [Strategy: Ask about the other person after giving information about yourself]

UNIT REVIEW: Podcast

Go online and listen to the podcast from the Unit Review.

1 Listen to the podcast. Choose *True* or *False*.

	True	False
1 Malcolm Gladwell thinks that anyone can be great at a skill.	☐	☐
2 Many scientists think that you need 10,000 (ten thousand) hours of practice to be great at a skill.	☐	☐
3 Professor Ortiz thinks that 10,000 hours can't always make you great at a skill.	☐	☐
4 Professor Ortiz and Malcom Gladwell both think that practice helps you become good at something.	☐	☐
5 Professor Ortiz thinks that natural ability isn't important for learning a skill.	☐	☐

2 Listen to the podcast again. Do the people talk about these skills?

	Yes	No
1 playing tennis	☐	☐
2 playing the guitar	☐	☐
3 painting	☐	☐
4 swimming	☐	☐
5 speaking a new language	☐	☐
6 playing basketball	☐	☐

3 Listen to the podcast again. Complete the sentences.

1 But now some scientists think this _____ true.

2 Practice is a _____ thing.

3 But 10,000 hours of swimming _____ make you the next Micheal Phelps!

4 Some people learn to speak a language _____.

5 And tall people are often _____ basketball.

LISTENING SKILL: Recognizing statements as questions ▶6.3

4 Listen to the excerpts from the podcast. Which statements are really questions? Choose *statement* or *question*.

	Statement	Question
1	☐	☐
2	☐	☐
3	☐	☐
4	☐	☐
5	☐	☐

DISCUSSION BOARD PREPARATION

5 Look at the Unit 6 Discussion Point. Read the questions in the prompt. Then read the reply. Is the quote true for the writer?

Unit 6 Review Discussion Point

1   Read the quote. Which activity is Michael Phelps great at?
    "Eat, sleep, and swim. That's all I can do."
    —Michael Phelps, selected from *Oxford Essential Quotations*, 5th ed., edited by Susan Ratcliffe
2   Do you think it's important to be great at one thing or to be good at many things? What do you want to be great at?
3   How can you become great at something?

Latest: Jasmine
Michael Phelps is great at swimming. I think it's important to be good at many things, not great at one thing. If you always practice one thing, you don't have time for other activities. That's boring. To become great at something, you need to practice a lot. You also need to have natural ability.

6   Overall, did the writer answer all the questions? If yes, explain. If no, what can she change?

7   Review the rubric. Use the rubric to give a score for the reply.
        Give points: 0 (not successful)–10 (successful).

Writing a Discussion Board Post	Points
The post answers the questions clearly and completely.	
The post uses adverbs of manner correctly.	
The post uses *can* and *can't* correctly.	
The post shows careful thinking about the topic.	
Sentences are complete and have correct punctuation.	
The post is long enough (50–60 words).	
Total	

WRITE YOUR POST

8   Read the quote. Do you think it's important to be great at one thing or to be good at many things? What do you want to be great at? How can you become great at something?

"Eat, sleep, and swim. That's all I can do."
—Michael Phelps, selected from
Oxford Essential Quotations, 5th ed.,
edited by Susan Ratcliffe

9   Use the rubric from Exercise 7 to score your post. Then improve your post.

 Go online to add your comments to the discussion board.

7 Reasons

Simple past of *be* ▶7.1

1 Choose *was* or *were*.

1 The weather *was / were* bad yesterday.

2 There *was / were* black clouds in the sky.

3 I *was / were* at home.

4 My roommates *was / were* at home, too.

5 We *was / were* inside all day.

2 Complete the paragraph with *was, wasn't, were,* or *weren't*.

This ¹_____ the first day of spring, but it ²_____ warm. It ³_____ only 9°C! There ⁴_____ classes because it ⁵_____ Saturday. My friends and I ⁶_____ at a café. It ⁷_____ very quiet. There ⁸_____ many people there because it ⁹_____ very early in the morning.

Simple past with *be*: Questions ▶7.2

3 Complete the *yes/no* questions and short answers.

1 A: _____ it warm yesterday?

   B: Yes, it _____.

2 A: _____ you at the beach?

   B: Yes, we _____.

3 A: _____ it fun?

   B: No, it _____.

4 A: _____ the sun out?

   B: No, it _____.

5 A: _____ the water cold?

   B: Yes, it _____.

4 Complete the questions with a question word and *was* or *were*.

1 A: _____ _____ Amelia Earhart's job?

   B: She was a pilot.

2 A: _____ _____ she from?

   B: Kansas, in the United States.

3 A: _____ _____ Amelia Earhart famous?

   B: Because she flew across the Atlantic.

4 A: _____ _____ her solo flight?

   B: In 1932.

5 A: _____ _____ people sad about?

   B: Amelia and her plane were lost.

5 Write the words in the correct order to make questions. Add punctuation.

1 you / where / on Friday night / were

   _____

2 why / was / angry / he

   _____

3 class / was / the / when

   _____

4 was / correct answer / what / the

   _____

5 were / they / why / at work / on Saturday

   _____

Simple past: Regular verbs ▶7.3

6 Complete the paragraph with past tense forms of the verbs in the box.

ask	~~help~~	start	end	plan

Last summer, my friends and I ¹_*helped*_ to raise money for a charity. We ²_____ a 10K road race, and we ³_____ a lot of people to run. The race ⁴_____ at a beach and ⁵_____ at another beach.

7 Choose the correct form of the verb.

1 I *play / played* tennis yesterday.

2 Ryan *likes / liked* eggs.

3 Liza *walk / walked* six kilometers this morning.

4 We *stay / stayed* home last Saturday night.

5 I *call / called* my sister after work yesterday.

Weather ▶7.1

1 Unscramble the letters to make weather words.

1 ratwerhe _____ 5 ndwi _____

2 inar _____ 6 wmra _____

3 ulcosd _____ 7 oth _____

4 olco _____ 8 dolc _____

2 Write the correct word from the box next to the temperature.

cold	cool	hot	warm

Temperature	Temperature word
32°C / 90°F	1
22°C / 72°F	2
10°C / 50°F	3
–5°C / 23°F	4

3 Match the first sentence in A with the second sentence in B.

A

1 The sun is out. ____

2 There's a lot of wind. ____

3 There's a lot of snow. ____

4 It's very hot. ____

5 There are clouds in the sky. ____

B

a We can't drive.

b I can't see the sun.

c Let's go sailing!

d It's a great day for the beach.

e I'd like a cold glass of water.

VOCABULARY DEVELOPMENT: Dates ▶7.2

4 Write the words for the ordinal numbers in the chart.

15th	fifteenth
21st	
30th	
42nd	
59th	

5 Write the months in the correct order.

April	February	July	November
August	January	March	October
December	June	May	September

1 _January_ 7 _____

2 _____ 8 _____

3 _____ 9 _____

4 _____ 10 _____

5 _____ 11 _____

6 _____ 12 _____

6 Write the years in words.

1 1975 _nineteen seventy-five_

2 2006 _____

3 1752 _____

4 2012 _____ or _____

5 1867 _____

6 1903 _____

7 Correct the mistakes in the **bold** phrases.

1 My birthday is **January twelfth, two thousands and eighteen.**

_____

2 Her first day of work was **thirtieth April, nineteen eighty seven.**

_____

3 In the United States, Thanksgiving is always **the third Thursday in november.**

_____

4 Our classes ended on **May fifteen.**

_____

5 My grandparents' wedding was on **August seconth, nineteen fifty-one.**

_____

6 Amelia Earhart was born on **July twenty-fourth, one thousand eight hundred and ninety seven.**

_____

1 Read the article. What is SAD?

SAD No More!

Before last year, I was usually sad in the winter. Then I learned that I had "seasonal affective disorder," or "SAD." People with SAD are sad in the winter, but they feel good in the spring and summer. Scientists think this is because they don't see enough sunlight. People with SAD live far from the equator. I live in Toronto, Canada. In the winter, the **weather** is very **cold** here, and we don't see much **sun**.

SAD is difficult, but there is help. I started running every morning, spending more time outdoors, and using a special "white lamp" in the winter. I sit near the lamp for two hours a day. These things helped a lot. Now I'm happy all year, even in December and January. I'm not "SAD"!

—adapted from *A Dictionary of Public Health* edited by John M. Last

2 Look at the photos. In which place are people most likely to have SAD? Why?

People are most likely to have SAD in photo ____ because _____.

3 Read the article again. Choose the correct word or phrase to complete the sentences.

1 The boy _____.

   a is sad in the winter   b is sometimes sad   c was sad in the winter

2 People with SAD are not _____ in the winter.

   a warm   b outdoors   c happy

3 People with SAD are _____ in the spring and summer.

   a hot   b happy   c cold

4 People with SAD usually live _____.

   a in northern places   b in southern places   c in cities

4 Read the article again. What can people with SAD do to feel better? Choose the correct answers.

____ 1 sleep a lot   ____ 3 drink coffee   ____ 5 sit near a special lamp

____ 2 exercise   ____ 4 sing   ____ 6 spend time outdoors

READING SKILL: Understanding *and* and *but* ▶7.2

5 Choose the best answer.

1 Yesterday it was hot, and _____.

  a there was a lot of sun   b there was a lot of snow   c there were gray clouds

2 The beach was beautiful, but _____.

  a there wasn't any snow   b the water was warm   c the water was very cold

3 December 21 was cold, and _____.

  a there was a lot of snow   b it was hot   c it was warm

4 It was very cold, but _____.

  a there was a lot of snow   b it was dark   c there was a lot of sun

5 There wasn't any sun, but _____.

  a it was hot   b it was cold   c there was a lot of rain

6 Read the sentences. Choose *and* or *but*.

1 I like cold weather, *and / but* I don't like snow.
2 Jorge is usually happy in the summer, *and / but* sad in the winter.
3 They traveled to Paris, *and / but* they visited a lot of museums.
4 We were at the beach yesterday, *and / but* we didn't swim.
5 Allie exercises a lot. She runs *and / but* she goes to the gym.
6 It was cold, *and / but* I didn't wear a jacket.

7 Look at the article in Exercise 1. Find three sentences with *and* and two sentences with *but*. Write them in the chart.

Sentences with *and*	Sentences with *but*
1	4
2	5
3	

8 In each sentence in Exercise 7, there are two ideas. Are the two ideas related or different?

1 _____   2 _____   3 _____   4 _____   5 _____

REAL-WORLD ENGLISH: Apologizing ▶7.4

1 Read the dialogues from the video. Find the places where: a) a person apologizes, and b) a person accepts an apology. Complete the chart with the people's words.

Apology	Acceptance of apology
1 Sorry about that. (Andy)	6
2	7
3	8
4	9
5	

Scene 1

Max: Uh, it was your turn to empty the bins last night. I mean, uh..the trash!

Andy: Oh. Sorry about that. I was sick…I mean…I am sick.

Max: It's OK. I can do it. Ah…there are tissues on the floor. You missed the basket!

Andy: Huh? Oops! Sorry about that. I was never good at basketball!

Scene 2

Andy: Hi Professor Lopez. So sorry I'm late.

Prof Lopez: What happened? You weren't in class.

Andy: I was at health services, and then I stopped to buy tea.

Max: I'm late, too. Sorry.

Prof Lopez: That's OK. Have a seat.

Andy: ACHOOO!

Andy: Oh, no…I'm really sorry!

Max: It's OK. It's OK.

Kevin: Aw, man! What is that? Tea? You don't drink tea!

Max: It's OK. I'll get it. Don't worry.

Andy: Thanks…

Max: Here…Take mine.

Prof Lopez: Don't worry, guys. That's just scrap paper!

2 Read the situations. Is each mistake big or small?

		Big	Small
1	You are 45 minutes late to meet your friend at a restaurant.	☐	☐
2	You bump into someone on the subway.	☐	☐
3	You phone rings loudly at a work meeting.	☐	☐
4	You spill water on your friend's phone. Now the phone doesn't work.	☐	☐

3 Write a conversation for each situation in Exercise 2.

1 A: _____

   B: _____

2 A: _____

   B: _____

3 A: _____

   B: _____

4 A: _____

   B: _____

UNIT REVIEW: Podcast

Go online and listen to the podcast from the Unit Review.

1 🔊 Listen to the podcast. Choose *True* or *False*.

	True	False
1 Dan learned a lot from his father.	☐	☐
2 Dan's father's family was rich.	☐	☐
3 Dan's father worked a lot.	☐	☐
4 Dan's father listened to people.	☐	☐
5 Dan's father was smart.	☐	☐
6 Today is Dan's birthday.	☐	☐

2 🔊 Listen to the podcast again. Complete the sentences.

1 In this episode, people are talking about _____ they are successful.

2 So, the _____ for my success is education.

3 He was my _____ teacher and my best one.

4 My dad stopped school after the _____ grade.

5 He _____ hard.

6 And he _____ about life from doing things.

7 And he also learned by listening to _____.

8 I think about him every day, especially today, June _____ – his birthday!

LISTENING SKILL: Listening for the beginning and ending of sentences ▶7.3

3 🔊 Listen to the pairs of sentences from the podcast. Write the word that begins the *second* sentence.

1 _____

2 _____

3 _____

4 _____

5 _____

DISCUSSION BOARD PREPARATION

4 Look at the Unit 7 Discussion Point. Read the questions in the prompt. Then read the reply. Does the writer agree with the quote?

_____

> **Unit 7 Review Discussion Point**
>
> 1   Read the quote. Do you agree? How can education help you to be successful?
>   *"If you want to know the reason why I'm standing here, it's because of education. I never cut class."*
>   —Michelle Obama, selected from *Oxford Essential Quotations*, 5th ed., edited by Susan Ratcliffe
> 2   How can education help you to be successful?
> 3   What other things can help you to be successful?
>
> > Latest: Omar
> > I agree with this quote. It is important to work hard in school. I was a good student in high school and college. I studied a lot, and I got good grades. Because of this, I now have a great job. An education also helps you to be a more interesting person. And it helps you to understand the world.

5 How did education help the writer?

6 Review the rubric. Use the rubric to give a score for the reply.
Give points: 0 (not successful)–10 (successful).

Writing a Discussion Board Post	Points
The post answers the questions clearly and completely.	
The post uses *was* and *were* correctly.	
The post uses the simple past of regular verbs correctly.	
The post shows careful thinking about the topic.	
Sentences are complete and have correct punctuation.	
The post is long enough (50–75 words).	
Total	

WRITE YOUR POST

7 Read the quote. Do you agree? How can education help you to be successful? What other things can help you to be successful?

 "If you want to know the reason why I'm standing here, it's because of education. I never cut class."
—Michelle Obama, selected from *Oxford Essential Quotations*, 5th ed., edited by Susan Ratcliffe

8 Use the rubric from Exercise 6 to score your post. Then improve your post.

 Go online to add your comments to the discussion board.

8 History

Simple past of irregular verbs ▶8.1

1 Write the simple past forms of the verbs.

1	take	_____	8	make	_____
2	do	_____	9	spend	_____
3	write	_____	10	have	_____
4	lose	_____	11	see	_____
5	buy	_____	12	think	_____
6	know	_____	13	begin	_____
7	get	_____	14	go	_____

2 Complete the paragraph about Maggie's trip to Tokyo with the simple past of verbs from Exercise 1.

Last summer I ¹_____ to Tokyo with two friends.

I ²_____ a lot of money, but it was a lot of fun! We

³_____ some interesting modern buildings. We

became friends with some Japanese students, and we

⁴_____ dinner at a restaurant with them one night.

I ⁵_____ hundreds of photos of our trip. You can

see them on my blog.

Simple past: Negative ▶8.2

3 These sentences about the paragraph in Exercise 2 are incorrect. Make the sentences negative, then correct the sentences.

1 Maggie went to Kyoto last summer.

   She didn't go to Kyoto. She went to Tokyo. _____

2 She traveled with her family.

   _____

3 They saw some old buildings.

   _____

4 They became friends with some Americans.

   _____

5 They had dinner at their friends' house.

   _____

6 Maggie took thousands of photos.

   _____

4 Correct the mistakes in the **bold** phrases.

1 He **didn't grows up** in China. _____

2 She **didn't has** any new friends. _____

3 They **didn't not live** in a big city. _____

4 I **didn't to like** high school very much. _____

5 He **dids not make** much money. _____

Simple past: *Yes/no* questions ▶8.3

5 Write the words in the correct order to make questions.

1 you / make / did / that dress

   _____?

2 they / live / in / did / a small town

   _____?

3 did / he / about / write / his trip

   _____?

4 wear / did / women / in the 1960s / jeans

   _____?

5 men / like to wear / did / in the 1950s / white T-shirts

   _____?

6 Write *yes/no* questions and short answers in the simple past about the paragraph in Exercise 2.

1 Maggie / go to Tokyo / last spring

   A: *Did Maggie go to Tokyo last spring?* _____

   B: *No, she didn't.* _____

2 she / spend / a lot of money

   A: _____?

   B: _____.

3 they / see / some interesting modern buildings

   A: _____?

   B: _____.

4 they / become friends / some Australian travelers

   A: _____?

   B: _____.

5 she / take photos of her trip / for her blog

   A: _____?

   B: _____.

VOCABULARY DEVELOPMENT:
Time expressions ▶8.1

1 Choose the correct word.

1 My grandfather was born *in / on* 1940.
2 *In / On* Saturday night, I wore a new dress.
3 Baggy jeans were popular *in / on* the 1990s.
4 My birthday is *in / on* February.
5 Maxi dresses were popular *in / on* the early 1970s.
6 We met three years *last / ago*.
7 Lucas was on vacation *last / ago* week.
8 Five months *last / ago,* I started college.

2 Correct the mistakes in the **bold** phrases.

1 Addie started working there **ago ten years.** _____

2 **In 1980s,** people wore bright colors. _____

3 Liz got a new job **the last year.** _____

4 My son was born **on the March 12.** _____

5 **In the 1990s late,** cell phones were very popular.
   _____

6 They got married **before six months.** _____

7 We stayed home **yesterday night.** _____

8 I was **last week sick.** _____

3 Write sentences putting the words in parenthesis in the correct place.

1 What did you do Saturday? (last)

   _____

2 I was born 1983. (in)

   _____

3 They went to Japan six years. (ago)

   _____

4 I started a new job month. (last)

   _____

5 My mother went to college early 1970s. (in the)

   _____

6 Monday we went to the theater. (on)

   _____

Clothes ▶8.3

4 Unscramble the letters to make clothes words.

1 ktjace _____ 5 hseos _____
2 sesrd _____ 6 thsri _____
3 srkit _____ 7 ath _____
4 stanp _____ 8 anjes _____

5 Choose the correct word.

1 My ears are cold. I need a *hat / jacket.*
2 It was hot yesterday. I wore a *jacket / T-shirt.*
3 I wore an expensive *dress / T-shirt* to my sister's wedding.
4 It was cool last night. I wore a *jacket / skirt.*
5 This pair of *pants / shoes* is too big for my feet.
6 Anna went to an important meeting at work. She wore *jeans / a skirt.*

6 Who is wearing the item of clothing? Write the name of the person (or people).

Nicole   **Lisa and Gilberto**

George   **Atsuko**   **Mary**

1 a hat _____
2 pants _____
3 a skirt _____
4 a T-shirt _____
5 a shirt _____
6 jeans _____
7 a dress _____
8 a jacket _____

7 What are you wearing today? What did you wear yesterday? Write the clothes (and colors) in the chart.

Today	Yesterday

READING SKILL: Scanning for specific information ▶8.3

1 Scan the article. Find six brands of sneakers. Write them below.

1 _____   4 _____

2 _____   5 _____

3 _____   6 _____

2 Scan the article again. Find the years. What happened in each year? Complete the chart.

Year	What happened?
	The U.S. Rubber Compay _____.
	Bill Bowerman and Phil Knight _____.
	Blue Ribbon Sports made _____.
	Blue Ribbon Sports got _____.
	_____ bought Converse.

The History of Sneakers

Home	About	Articles

These days, people wear them everywhere! But how did sneakers begin?

In the late eighteenth century, people first wore shoes with rubber bottoms. They didn't have a left and right foot! In 1917, the U.S. Rubber Company made more comfortable rubber shoes called Keds. These were the first sneakers. They were only for sports.

Today, the four biggest sneaker companies in the world are Nike, Adidas, Puma, and Asics. Nike makes my favorite shoes.

A coach, Bill Bowerman, and an athlete, Phil Knight, started Nike in Portland, Oregon, in 1964. Its first name was *Blue Ribbon Sports*. They didn't make shoes. They sold shoes that other companies made. That changed in the early 1970s. In 1971, the company made a soccer shoe called *Nike*. The name came from Greek mythology.

In 1978, the company got a new name: *Nike*. Did you know that Nike owns other shoe companies? They bought Converse in 2003.

—adapted from *A Dictionary of Sports Studies* by Alan Tomlinson

READING: Practice

3 Read the article on page 52. Write *sneakers* (and the year sneakers were first made) in the correct place on the timeline.

Timeline of inventions

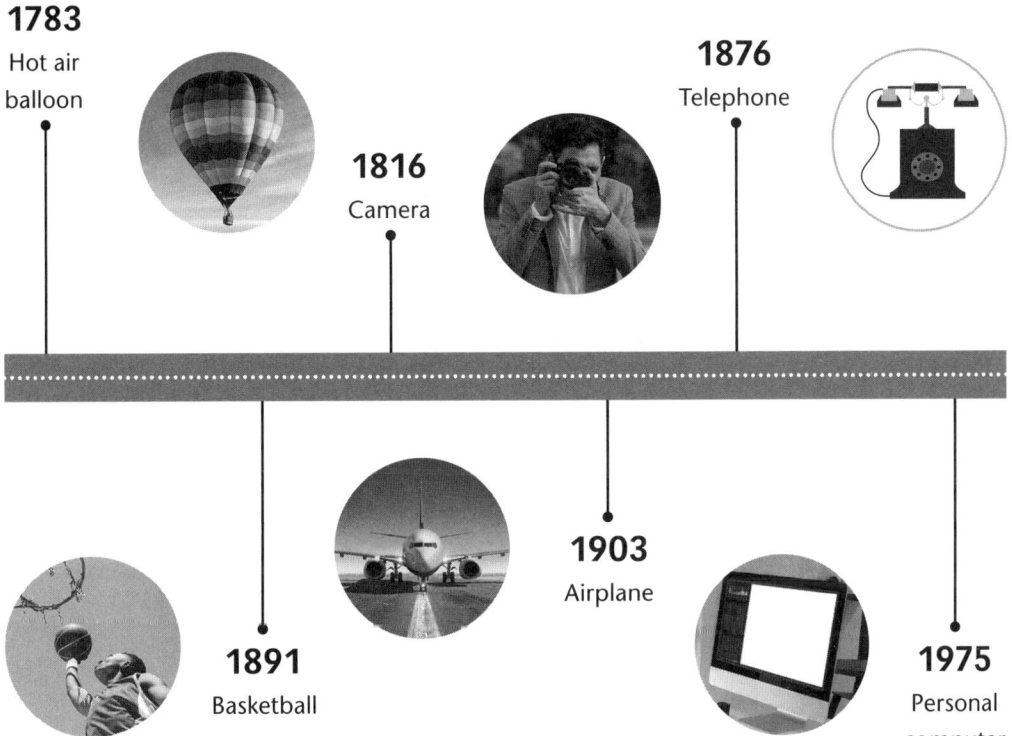

1783
Hot air balloon

1816
Camera

1876
Telephone

1903
Airplane

1891
Basketball

1975
Personal computer

4 Choose *True* or *False*.

		True	False
1	Keds didn't have a right and left foot.	☐	☐
2	In the early twentieth century, people wore sneakers only for sports.	☐	☐
3	The U.S. Rubber Company made the first sneaker.	☐	☐
4	Three people started Nike.	☐	☐
5	Nike's first name was Blue Ribbon Sports.	☐	☐
6	In 1964, Nike started making shoes.	☐	☐
7	The name *Nike* came from a Greek island.	☐	☐

REAL-WORLD ENGLISH: Reacting to news ▶8.4

1 Read the dialogues from the video. Choose the best reactions.

Scene 1

Max:	You're in a good mood.
Andy:	Yeah! I passed my big history test!
Max:	Really? [1]*Oh, congratulations! Brilliant! / Oh, that's nice…* [2]*Good. / Wow!* You were so worried about that.
Andy:	I know. I studied all month.

Scene 2

Max:	Hi. How's it going?
Andy:	Uh, we just got tickets home for winter break.
Max:	Oh…[3]*That's too bad. / That's…that's cool.* Wait…we?
Kevin:	Yeah. We ride the train together.
Max:	[4]*Oh…cool. / Wow! That's great!*
Kevin:	What about you, Max? London?
Max:	No. I can't go home. Uh, the tickets are very expensive right now.
Andy:	[5]*Cool! / Oh, no! That's too bad.*
Kevin:	Yeah.
Max:	Yeah. Oh, well. I won a free pass to the art museum. Uh…I can use it during break!
Kevin/Andy:	[6]*Congratulations! / Oh, I'm sorry!*

2 Number the news in order: 1 (best news)–5 (worst news).

_____ Today is my birthday.

_____ I can't find my phone. I think it's in the taxi!

_____ We have a new baby.

_____ I broke my leg.

_____ I made a website.

3 Complete the conversations with an appropriate reaction.

1 A: Today is my birthday.

    B: _____

2 A: I can't find my phone. I think it's in the taxi!

    B: _____

3 A: We have a new baby.

    B: _____

4 A: I broke my leg.

    B: _____

5 A: I made a website.

    B: _____

LISTENING SKILL: Using visuals to help you understand ▶8.1

@ Go online and listen to the podcast from the Unit Review.

1 ◀》 Look at the photo. What do you think is the topic of the podcast?

a the Ford Model T car

b today's cars

c learning to drive

2 ◀》 Listen to the podcast. How is the car the same as today's cars? How is it different?

Same	Different

UNIT REVIEW: Podcast

3 ◀》 Listen to the podcast again. Which words describe the Model T?

☐ expensive   ☐ comfortable   ☐ safe

☐ quiet   ☐ noisy   ☐ fun

4 ◀》 Listen to the podcast again. Choose the correct word to complete each sentence.

1 The Model T changed _____.

a drivers   b people   c the world

2 In 1925, the Model T was _____.

a $300   b $500   c $800

3 _____ of people bought Model Ts.

a hundreds   b thousands   c millions

4 The Model T was _____ in the winter.

a comfortable   b cold   c safe

5 The Model T didn't have _____.

a windows   b a roof   c a radio

DISCUSSION BOARD PREPARATION

5 Look at the Unit 8 Discussion Point. Read the questions in the prompt. Then read the reply. Does the writer agree with the quote?

_____

Unit 8 Review Discussion Point

1   Read the quote. Do you think the past is very different from the present? How?
    "The past is a foreign country: they do things differently there."
    —L. P. Hartley, selected from the *Oxford Dictionary of Quotations*, 8th ed.,
    edited by Elizabeth Knowles

2   Think of a year in the past. How are things different today? What things are better? What things are worse?

Latest: Ji-yeon
I don't think the past is very different from the present. Think about life in 1750. Some things are better today: We have cars, phones, and computers. Some things are worse, like traffic and pollution. But the important things are the same. in 1750, people had problems with their friends and family; they got sick; maybe they didn't like their jobs. We have the same problems today. And the same things make us happy.

6 What does the writer say is the same about the past and the present? What is different?

7 Review the rubric. Use the rubric to give a score for the reply.
Give points: 0 (not successful)–10 (successful).

Writing a Discussion Board Post	Points
The post answers the questions clearly and completely.	
The post uses simple past of irregular verbs correctly.	
The post uses the negative form of verbs in the simple past correctly.	
The post shows careful thinking about the topic.	
Sentences are complete and have correct capitalization and punctuation.	
The post is long enough (50–75 words).	
Total	

WRITE YOUR POST

8 Read the quote. Do you think the past is very different from the present? How? Think of a year in the past. How are things different today? What things are better? What things are worse?

"The past is a foreign country: they do things differently there."
—L. P. Hartley, selected from the *Oxford Dictionary of Quotations*, 8th ed., edited by Elizabeth Knowles

9 Use the rubric from Exercise 7 to score your post. Then improve your post.

 Go online to add your comments to the discussion board.

9 Comforts

Countable and uncountable nouns ▶9.1

1 Write the words in the correct column.

| apple | egg | onion | tea | vegetable |
| bread | fruit | pasta | tomato | water |

Countable	Uncountable

2 Complete the sentences with *a*, *an*, *some*, or *any*.

1 I'd like _____ water, please.

2 We don't have _____ onions.

3 Would you like ___ ___ apple?

4 Eat _____ vegetables!

5 I don't want _____ coffee.

Quantifiers: *Much / many / a lot* ▶9.2

3 Choose the correct word.

1 Lily doesn't drink *much* / *many* coffee.

2 We eat *much* / *a lot* of fruit.

3 Please get *much* / *some* bananas.

4 We don't go to *much* / *many* restaurants.

5 They don't have *much* / *many* money.

4 Write questions with *How much* or *How many*.

1 hours / you / work / every week

   _____

2 sisters / he / have

   _____

3 bread / you / eat / every day

   _____

4 friends / you / have

   _____

5 rice / they / eat / every week

   _____

5 Correct the mistakes in the **bold** phrases. One sentence is correct.

1 **How much apples** would you like? _____

2 We don't have **many milk**. _____

3 They eat **much bread**. _____

4 We had **much fun** last night. _____

5 **How many chairs** do we need? _____

6 The tent has **somes chairs**. _____

Would like: Requests and offers ▶9.3

6 Write the words in the correct order to make requests and offers. Add punctuation.

1 you / like / would / coffee / some

   _____

2 to eat / where / like / you / would

   _____

3 like / we'd / to take / to our hotel / a taxi

   _____

4 to meet / would / like / you / at the restaurant

   _____

5 like / I'd / please / some coffee

   _____

7 Match the responses below to the offers and requests in Exercise 6.

___3___ a I can call one for you.

_____ b How about that new pizza place?

_____ c Yes, please.

_____ d No, let's meet at the hotel.

_____ e Would you like milk in it?

VOCABULARY DEVELOPMENT:
Food and drink ▶9.1

1 Write the words in the correct column.

bread	eggs	fruit	milk	tea
coffee	fish	meat	rice	vegetables

Foods	Drinks

2 Choose the correct word.

1 We don't buy *fish / eggs* at the store. We get them from our chickens.

2 Apples are my favorite *vegetable / fruit*.

3 Babies drink a lot of *tea / milk*.

4 Carrots and lettuce are *vegetables / fruits*.

5 I had *coffee / milk* at 8 p.m. Now I can't sleep.

6 Joanna is a vegetarian. She doesn't eat *meat / bread*.

Furniture ▶9.2

3 Unscramble the letters to make furniture words.

1 firgreretar   _____

2 edb   _____

3 lpam   _____

4 ofsa   _____

5 VT   _____

6 rciha   _____

7 dkse   _____

8 ltbea   _____

4 Write words from Exercise 3.

1 You sleep on this. _____

2 You eat on this. _____

3 You watch this. _____

4 You work at this. _____

5 One person sits on this. _____

6 This helps you see. _____

7 Two or three people can sit on this. _____

8 You put food in this. _____

5 Look at the picture. Complete the sentences. You can use a word more than once.

1 There are two _____ in the living room.

2 There is a book on a _____ in the living room.

3 There is a TV on the _____ in the living room.

4 There is a _____ next to the sofas in the living room.

Descriptive adjectives ▶9.3

6 Match the sentence in A with the sentence in B.

A

1 I'm really **tired**. ____

2 I'm **hungry**. ____

3 Don't go to that restaurant. ____

4 Thank you! ____

5 I'm not **ready**. ____

6 The stores aren't **open** today. ____

B

a Their food is **terrible**.

b Is there any food in the refrigerator?

c That was an **excellent** dinner.

d I was up late last night.

e It's a holiday.

f I need five more minutes.

7 Complete the sentences with **bold** words from Exercise 6.

1 That was an _____ soccer game. Both teams played well.

2 Are you _____? Do you want some fruit?

3 The weather was _____ today! It rained and rained...

4 Are you _____ to go? I don't want to be late.

5 Nate went home early because he was very _____.

6 The supermarket is _____ from 7 a.m. to 11 p.m

READING SKILL: Understanding the organization of a text:
Topic sentences ▶9.2

1 Before you read, scan the article to find the topic sentences. What is the topic sentence of each paragraph?

Paragraph 1

____ After a hard day, do you like to have some ice cream?

____ These are "comfort foods."

____ But not all comfort foods are sweet: soup and mac and cheese are also comfort foods for many people.

Paragraph 3

____ First, comfort foods make us remember happy times and people we love.

____ When you were young, maybe your parents gave you chicken soup.

____ And you feel good!

Paragraph 4

____ Second, some comfort foods—like chocolate—have chemicals in them.

____ These chemicals make us feel happy and relaxed.

Comfort Eating

After a hard day, do you like to have some ice cream? Or chocolate? These are "comfort foods." A comfort food makes you feel good. Chocolate, cake, donuts, and ice cream are popular comfort foods. But not all comfort foods are sweet: Soup and pasta are also comfort foods for many people.

There are two reasons that comfort foods make us feel good.

First, comfort foods make us remember happy times and people we love. When you were young, maybe your parents gave you chicken soup. Now, when you eat chicken soup, you think about your family. And you feel good!

Second, some comfort foods—like chocolate—have chemicals in them. These chemicals make us feel happy and relaxed.

—adapted from *A Dictionary of Food and Fitness,* 2nd ed., by Michael Kent

2 Do you understand the meaning of the topic sentences? If not, use a dictionary to help you understand. Make notes in the chart.

New words	Meanings

READING: Practice

3 Read the article on page 59. Choose *True* or *False*.

		True	False
1	Comfort foods are always sweet.	☐	☐
2	Everyone has the same comfort foods.	☐	☐
3	Comfort foods make us feel good for three reasons.	☐	☐
4	Comfort foods make us think about places and people we love.	☐	☐
5	Comfort foods have chemicals.	☐	☐
6	The chemicals can make you relaxed.	☐	☐
7	Comfort foods make us happy.	☐	☐

4 Read the article again. Choose the popular comfort foods.

 ☐
 ☐
 ☐
 ☐
 ☐
 ☐

REAL-WORLD ENGLISH: Accepting and rejecting offers ▶9.4

1 Complete the dialogue from Scene 2 of the video with words from the box.

| don't really | interesting | really | thanks | try some | would you |

Scene 2

Max: And now, from the shop downtown: Steak and kidney pie! Mmm mmm.

¹_____ like to try some?

Andy: Uh...No ²_____. I ³_____ like...kidney.

Max: Oh, come on. Just taste it.

Andy: Oh...OK. Mmm...It's good. And I have something very American.

Max: Oh?

Andy: My comfort food.

Max: Hmm. That looks...uh...⁴_____.

Andy: Mac and cheese! Would you like to ⁵_____?

Max: Not ⁶_____. I don't usually eat pasta with...orange cheese.

Andy: Aw...just a little?

2 In Scene 2, why do Andy and Max reject the offers? Write their reasons in the chart.

Person	Reason for rejecting the offer
Andy	
Max	

3 What are some other reasons you can give to reject an offer of food or drink?

1 _____

2 _____

3 _____

4 _____

4 Write two conversations with offers.

1 Your friend: _____ [A friend offers you some food or drink.]

You: _____ [Accept the offer politely.]

2 Your friend: _____ [A friend offers you some food or drink.]

You: _____ [Reject the offer politely. Give a reason.]

Your friend: _____ [Your friend tells you more about the food or

drink and offers again.]

You: _____ [Accept the offer.]

UNIT REVIEW: Podcast

 Go online and listen to the podcast from the Unit Review.

1 🔊 Listen to the podcast. What is the topic of the podcast?

a   what makes people happy

b   beautiful places

c   weekend activities

2 🔊 Listen to the podcast again. Complete the sentences.

1   Cory's small *tent / house / apartment* makes him happy.

2   He goes there on *weekends / vacations / holidays*.

3   He likes it because it's *green / beautiful / comfortable* and quiet.

4   There is *a lot of / not much / expensive* furniture.

LISTENING SKILL: Listening for detail ▶9.1

3 🔊 Listen to the podcast again. Choose **one or more** correct answers.

1   What furniture is in Cory's favorite place?

   a   a table   b   three chairs

   c   a sofa   d   two beds

2   How does Cory usually feel when he arrives there?

   a   hungry   b   happy

   c   tired   d   terrible

3   What does he eat there?

   a   fruit   b   eggs

   c   pasta   d   bread

4   What does he do there?

   a   read   b   walk

   c   watch TV   d   swim

DISCUSSION BOARD PREPARATION

4 Look at the Unit 9 Discussion Point. Read the questions in the prompt. Then read the reply. Is the quote true for the writer? Why or why not?

Unit 9 Review Discussion Point

1 Read the quote. Do you agree? In your opinion, what makes a house comfortable?
"A comfortable house is a great source of happiness."
—Sydney Smith, selected from *Oxford Essential Quotations*, 5th ed., edited by Susan Ratcliffe

2 What is a great source of happiness for you?

Latest: Pedro
I don't agree with the quote. I don't spend many time at home, so having a comfortable house isn't important to me. For me, a great source of happiness is soccer. I play a lot of soccer with my friends. We usually play on Tuesday evenings and Saturday mornings. On weekends, I watch professional soccer on TV. My favorite team is Barcelona!

5 What is a great source of happiness for the writer?

6 Review the rubric. Use the rubric to give a score for the reply.
Give points: 0 (not successful)–10 (successful).

Writing a Discussion Board Post	Points
The post answers the questions clearly and completely.	
The post uses countable and uncountable nouns correctly.	
The post uses quantifiers (*much, many, a lot*) correctly.	
The post shows careful thinking about the topic.	
Sentences are complete and have correct punctuation.	
The post is long enough (50–75 words).	
Total	

WRITE YOUR POST

7 Read the quote. Do you agree? If you agree, answer this question: In your opinion, what makes a house comfortable? If you don't agree, answer this question: What is a great source of happiness for you?

"A comfortable house is a great source of happiness."
—Sydney Smith, selected from *Oxford Essential Quotations*,
5th ed., edited by Susan Ratcliffe

8 Use the rubric from Exercise 6 to score your post. Then improve your post.

 Go online to add your comments to the discussion board.

10 Adventures

1 Find the object pronouns in the paragraph.

My cousin lives in Egypt, and last summer I visited him. Egypt is a very interesting place. I loved it! First, I spent some time in Cairo. My cousin gave me a tour of the city. Next, we went to the Pyramids of Giza. First, I saw them from the outside. Then a tour guide took us inside. They were amazing!

2 Write the object pronouns from Exercise 1 in the chart. Write the words they talk about.

Object pronoun	Word the object pronoun talks about
him	my cousin

3 Complete the sentences with the correct object pronoun.

1 The Matterhorn is a mountain in Switzerland. I climbed _____ last summer.

2 My grandparents live two hours from me. I visit _____ once a month.

3 Do you want to see the city? I can give _____ a tour.

4 He's a great actor. I saw _____ in his new movie.

5 We went to our friends' house last night. They made a nice dinner for _____.

6 My father bought _____ a suitcase for my birthday.

Comparative adjectives: Short forms ▶10.2

4 Write the comparative form of the adjectives.

1 happy _____
2 safe _____
3 pretty _____
4 nice _____
5 big _____
6 early _____

5 Write sentences with the comparative form of the adjective.

1 this summer / hot / last summer
   This summer is hotter than last summer.

2 this photo / dark / that one
   _____

3 a sea / deep / a lake
   _____

4 my brother / old / my sister
   _____

5 forests / pretty / deserts
   _____

6 planes / safe / cars
   _____

Comparative adjectives: Long and irregular forms ▶10.3

6 Complete the sentences with the comparative form of the adjective and *than*.

1 The sculpture garden is _more interesting than_ the history museum. (interesting)

2 Staying in a hotel is _____ camping. (expensive)

3 Camping is _____ staying in a hotel. (exciting)

4 This vacation is _____ the one we took last year! (good)

5 Today I feel _____ I did yesterday. (bad)

6 The airport is _____ the train station from our hotel. (far)

7 Correct the mistakes in the **bold** phrases. One sentence is correct.

1 This restaurant is **badder than** the one we went to last night. _____

2 The hotels near the beach are **more expensiver than** the ones downtown. _____

3 The movie is **more boring** the book. _____

4 The city is **more beautiful in** the sea. _____

5 Driving is **more dangerous than** flying. _____

Geography ▶10.1

1 Unscramble the letters to make geography words.

1 rganed   g_____
2 fstore   f_____
3 laglive   v_____
4 sredet   d_____
5 ntoasmuin   m_____
6 diseytoucnr   c____ __
7 keal   l_____
8 ase   s_____

2 Choose the correct words.

1 *A village / The countryside* doesn't have many houses.
2 The *desert / village* doesn't have any trees.
3 In the *mountains / desert,* there is sometimes snow in the summer.
4 Vegetables grow in a *garden / sea.*
5 A *sea / village* is a small town.
6 A *forest / lake* has a lot of trees.

VOCABULARY DEVELOPMENT:
Adjectives ▶10.2

3 Match the sentence in A with the sentence in B.

A

____ 1 I saw a scary movie tonight.
____ 2 Cave diving is dangerous.
____ 3 The sun is very bright today.
____ 4 It's a very pretty sea.
____ 5 The lake isn't very deep.
____ 6 This is an interesting book.

B

a Do you want to read it?
b Now I can't sleep!
c Remember to wear sunglasses.
d I took a lot of pictures of it.
e You can see the bottom from the boat.
f Don't do it alone.

4 Write the words in the correct order to make sentences.

1 lake / cool / is / the
_____

2 saw / we / mountains / beautiful / some
_____.

3 went / we / vacation / exciting / on an
_____

4 those sculptures / interesting / are
_____

5 a / cave / went into / deep / they
_____

Vacation ▶10.3

5 Complete the sentences with words from the box.

break	suitcase	summer
trip	vacation	winter

1 We stayed home for our _____. It was very relaxing.
2 Every morning at 10:00, I stop working and take a coffee _____.
3 _____ is my favorite time of year because I love hot weather.
4 In the _____, Martin skis every weekend.
5 Every year, I take a two-week _____ with my sisters and brothers. We usually go somewhere warm.
6 You don't need to pack a big _____.

6 Write the words from the box in Exercise 5 in the correct row. You can use words more than once.

take a	
go on a	
go in the	
travel in the	

READING SKILL: Recognizing and understanding
subject-verb-object sentences ▶10.2

1 Read the article. Find the verbs.

Costa Rica Adventure

Home | About | Articles

Do you want an exciting vacation? Visit Costa Rica! Costa Rica has beautiful mountains, forests, and beaches. And the people are very friendly.

For a stress-free trip, travel with PV tours. We do all the work. You can relax! A PV traveler wrote:

"Our tour guides took us to some great places. On the first day, we did a ropes course. We climbed high up into the trees. From there, we saw beautiful mountains. It was safe, but a little scary. It was also a lot of fun!

The next day, we rode horses on a pretty beach. On the third day, we walked around a cute village and went shopping. I bought some coffee for my friends at home.

It was an amazing vacation. Traveling with PV tours is more fun, more interesting, and easier than traveling alone!"

—adapted from *A Guide to Countries of the World*, 4th ed., by Christopher Riches and Peter Stalker

2 Look at these sentences from the article. Find the subject, verb, and object in each sentence. Write them in chart.

1 We do all the work.
2 Our tour guides took us to some great places.
3 On the first day, we did a ropes course.
4 From there, we saw beautiful mountains.
5 The next day, we rode horses on a pretty beach.
6 I bought some coffee for my friends at home.

Sentence	Subject	Verb	Object
1			
2			
3			
4			
5			
6			

READING: Practice

3 Which activities does the writer say you can do in Costa Rica? Check the boxes.

1   ride horses

2   go shopping

3   go cave diving

4   visit a village

5   go to the beach

6   watch sports

4 Choose the answer that is NOT correct.

1   Costa Rica is a good place to visit because _____.

a   it is exciting

b   it isn't expensive

c   the people are nice

2   Costa Rica has _____.

a   a desert

b   mountains

c   forests

3   PV Tours is _____

a   an adventure travel company

b   a bus company

c   a good company

4   The ropes course was _____

a   fun

b   scary

c   dangerous

5   On the third day, they _____.

a   visited a village

b   went to some stores

c   drank coffee

6   The traveler thought that traveling with PV tours was _____.

a   boring

b   fun

c   easy

REAL-WORLD ENGLISH: Giving opinions and making suggestions ▶10.4

1 Complete the dialogue from the video with words from the box.

about	hmm	what	like	thanks	think

Max: Wild west? What, like, cowboys?

Andy: Mmm...I mean, Las Vegas!

Max: Las Vegas? No ¹_____. What ²_____ somewhere quieter and more relaxing, like a ranch?

Andy: Well, I think a ranch sounds kind of boring. Come on, Vegas is a fun city.

Max: I can ³_____ of nicer places to go. ⁴_____ about...the Grand Canyon? I really want to go there.

Andy: Everyone visits the Grand Canyon. It's one of the most popular vacation spots. It's always crowded.

Max: How could it be crowded? It's one of the biggest parks in the country!

Andy: OK. True. ⁵_____.

Max: Well, I'd really ⁶_____ to ride horses at a ranch. And draw!

2 Find the responses to suggestions in the dialogue. Write them in the correct column.

Positive opinions	Negative opinions
1	1
	2
	3
	4

3 Make a list of exciting things you can do this weekend.

1 _____ 2 _____ 3 _____

4 Complete the conversation between two friends.

A: _____

[Make a suggestion of something exciting to do this weekend.]

B: _____

[Respond with a negative opinion.]

A: _____

[Make a different suggestion.]

B: _____

[Respond with another negative opinion. Then make a suggestion.]

A: _____

[Respond with a positive opinion.]

UNIT REVIEW: Podcast

 Go online and listen to the podcast from the Unit Review.

1 Listen to the podcast. Look at the photos. What kind of person are the speakers talking about?

2 Listen to the podcast again. Choose the correct answers.

1 Some people like exciting activities. They like to _____.

   a   climb mountains   b   stay at home

2 Other people like to _____.

   a   do rope courses   b   feel safe

3 When people do dangerous activities, their body makes _____.

   a   adrenaline and dopamine   b   water

4 These things make people feel _____.

   a   good   b   angry

5 Some people need more _____ to make them feel good.

   a   comfort food   b   excitement

LISTENING SKILL: Listening for the number of words in a sentence ▶ 10.1

3 Listen to the sentences from the podcast. How many words are in each sentence? Write the number.

1 ___   2 ___   3 ___   4 ___   5 ___   6 ___

DISCUSSION BOARD PREPARATION

4 Look at the Unit 10 Discussion Point. Read the questions in the prompt. Then read the reply. Does the writer agree with the quote?

_____

Unit 10 Review Discussion Point

1   Read the quote. Do you agree?
     "There is only one thing in the world worse than being talked about, and that is not being talked about."
     —Oscar Wilde, selected from *Oxford Essential Quotations*, 5th ed., edited by Susan Ratcliffe
2   Write your own quote following the same structure: "There is only one thing in the world worse than…, and that is…" Explain your quote.

Latest: **Emily**
I don't agree with this quote. I don't want people to talk about me! Only people who is bored talk about other people. My own quote is, "There is only one thing in the world worse than being scared, and that is being bored." I hates sitting at home and doing nothing. I'm happier when I'm busy. I'm usually out of the house, doing things with friends. When I'm home, I cook, read, or watch movies.

5   What is the writer's quote? Why is that quote true for her?

6   Review the rubric. Use the rubric to give a score for the reply.
        Give points: 0 (not successful)–10 (successful).

Writing a Discussion Board Post	Points
The post answers the questions clearly and completely.	
Sentences have subject-verb agreement.	
The post uses comparative adjectives correctly.	
The post shows careful thinking about the topic.	
Sentences are complete and have correct punctuation.	
The post is long enough (50–75 words).	
Total	

WRITE YOUR POST

7   Read the quote. Do you agree? Write your own quote following the same structure: "There is only one thing in the world worse than…, and that is…" Explain your quote.

 *"There is only one thing in the world worse than being talked about, and that is not being talked about."*
—Oscar Wilde, selected from *Oxford Essential Quotations*, 5th ed., edited by Susan Ratcliffe

8   Use the rubric from Exercise 6 to score your post. Then improve your post.

Go online to add your comments to the discussion board.

11 Learning

GRAMMAR

Present continuous: Positive and negative ▶11.1

1 Complete the sentences with the positive or negative present continuous form of the verb. Use contractions.

1 I _____ how to be a coach. (learn)
2 We _____ on a difficult problem. Can you help us? (work)
3 They _____ about the video they saw. (talk)
4 Jason _____ any science classes. (not / take)
5 We _____ about the present continuous in English class. (learn)
6 Our teacher _____ quietly. I can't hear her. (speak)
7 They _____. (not / study)
8 I _____ for a new job. (not / look)

2 Correct the mistakes in the **bold** phrases.

1 I **talking** on the phone right now. _____
2 We **are take** a Spanish class. _____
3 She **are writing** an example on the board. _____
4 They **aren't not listening** to the teacher. _____
5 He **is showings** us how to do the problem. _____

Using -ing forms as subjects ▶11.2

3 Write the -ing form of the correct verbs from the box to complete the sentences.

look	say	study	take	watch

1 _____ grammar helps me speak English better.
2 For me, _____ videos is a good way to learn.
3 _____ at pictures helps visual learners.
4 _____ a short study break every hour is a good idea.
5 _____ a word five times can help you remember it.

4 Find the subject in each sentence.

1 I'm taking four classes right now.
2 Learning about science is very interesting.
3 Kinesthetic learners don't like sitting in a chair for a long time.
4 Looking at examples can help you understand something.
5 The students are listening to their teacher.

Present continuous: Questions ▶11.3

5 Write the words in the correct order to make questions.

1 you / a video / watching / are
_____?
2 is / he / staying / where
_____?
3 talking about / what / are / they
_____?
4 about me / they / are / talking
_____?
5 why / she / is / going home
_____?

6 Write questions with the present continuous. Then complete the answers.

1 you / work on / the math problem
   A: _Are you working on the math problem?_
   B: _Yes, I am._
2 where / you / go
   A: _____?
   B: _____ to class.
3 what / you / learn about / in English class
   A: _____?
   B: _____ about how to make suggestions.
4 he / study / Japanese history
   A: _____?
   B: No, _____.
5 she / teach / that class
   A: _____?
   B: Yes, _____.

Unit 11 Learning

VOCABULARY DEVELOPMENT:
Study collocations ▶11.1

1 Write the words from the box in the correct column in the chart.

a break	a mistake	homework	well
a class	a test	notes	

make	take	do

2 Match the beginning of the sentence in A with the ending in B.

A

1 I'm tired. I want to take ____

2 You made a ____

3 Victor does ____

4 Please try ____

5 I usually take ____

6 We need to write ____

7 Ally likes learning ____

8 I always stay up late the night before I take ____

B

a mistake. The correct answer is 17.

b about science.

c a test.

d homework every night from 7 to 9.

e to arrive to class on time.

f a paper for history class.

g notes in a notebook, not on a laptop.

h a break.

3 Circle the correct word to complete each sentence.

1 This class is long. I need to _____ a break.

   a make   b take   c do

2 When I'm tired, I often _____ a mistake.

   a make   b take   c do

3 Sarah wants to _____ well at her job.

   a make   b take   c do

4 We study hard before we _____ a test.

   a make   b take   c do

5 Do you want to _____ homework together?

   a make   b take   c do

6 My classmates _____ really helpful notes.

   a make   b take   c do

Education ▶11.2

4 Unscramble the letters to make education words.

1 eebmerrm   r_____

2 hsow   s_____

3 dtnuaersdn   u_____

4 vome   m_____

5 npilxae   e_____

6 eepxmal   e_____

7 lmrobpe   p_____

5 Complete the sentences with words from Exercise 4.

1 I didn't _____ the ending of the movie. Can you please _____ it to me?

2 When you are studying, take a break every hour. Get up and _____!

3 This math _____ is easy.

4 Do you _____ where we parked the car?

5 Can you _____ me how to do that on my computer?

6 Our book gives an _____ for every exercise. That helps us understand how to do it.

Work ▶11.3

6 Look at the **bold** words in the phrases. Write them in the correct column in the chart.

Nouns	Verbs	Adjectives

1 go to **meetings**
2 **make** (people) happy
3 have a **part-time** job
4 learn new **skills**
5 work for a large **company**
6 **look** for a new job
7 work in an **office**
8 **help** people

7 Complete the paragraph with words from the box.

company	learn	make	meetings	part-time
help	looking	makes	office	skills

Rachel has a ¹_____ job at a small ²_____. She works in an ³_____ from 9 to 5 on Mondays, Wednesdays, and Fridays. She writes reports and goes to a lot of ⁴_____. She ⁵_____ a lot of money, but she doesn't like her job very much. She is ⁶_____ for a new job. She wants to ⁷_____ people and ⁸_____ them happy. It isn't easy to find a job. She needs to ⁹_____ some new ¹⁰_____ first.

READING SKILL: Skimming ▶11.2

1 Choose the correct answers to complete the sentences about skimming.

1 When you skim, you _____.
   a read a text carefully
   b look at a text quickly
   c take notes on a text

2 Skimming helps you to _____.
   a find the most important ideas
   b understand new words
   c remember a lot of details

3 You skim when you want to _____.
   a remember a lot about the text
   b study for a test
   c learn what a text is about

4 Skimming _____.
   a takes a lot of time
   b doesn't take much time
   c sometimes *a* and sometimes *b*

2 Skim the article for the main idea. Choose the correct main idea below.

☐ 1 You need to study a lot before a test.
☐ 2 Sleeping helps you learn.
☐ 3 People dream when they are in REM sleep.
☐ 4 SWS sleep helps you learn how to ride a bike.
☐ 5 You need REM and NREM sleep.

Sleep Smart

The author John Steinbeck once said, "It is a common experience that a problem difficult at night is resolved in the morning after the committee of sleep has worked on it."

He meant this: Sleeping helps us learn and remember things. These days, many scientists are studying the connection between sleep and learning.

There are two kinds of sleep: REM (rapid eye movement) and NREM (non-rapid eye movement).

In REM sleep, you dream a lot. In NREM sleep, you don't dream.

Scientists think that REM and NREM sleep help you learn different things. Are you studying for a test? REM sleep is important for that. It helps you remember facts, like who the president of Brazil is. Are you learning to program a computer? Then NREM is your friend! NREM sleep helps you remember how to do things.

—adapted from *The Oxford Companion to the Body* by Colin Blakemore and Sheila Jennett
—Steinbeck quote is from *Oxford Essential Quotations*, 5th ed., edited by Susan Ratcliffe

READING: Practice

3 Read the article again. Choose *True* or *False*.

	True	False
1 John Steinbeck thought that sleep wasn't important.	☐	☐
2 Scientists are studying sleep and learning.	☐	☐
3 REM and NREM are two kinds of sleep.	☐	☐
4 In NREM sleep, you dream a lot.	☐	☐
5 REM sleep helps you remember how to do things.	☐	☐
6 Sleeping a lot can help you do well in school.	☐	☐

4 Read the article again. What kind of sleep helps you learn each thing? Write *REM* or *NREM*.

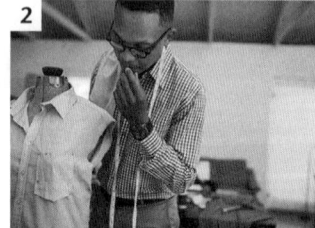

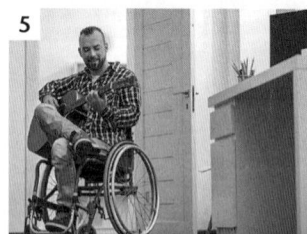

1 how to play chess _____

2 how to make clothes _____

3 who has the world record for running a mile _____

4 what the weather was like yesterday _____

5 how to play the guitar _____

6 the age of the Taj Mahal _____

REAL-WORLD ENGLISH: Turn taking ▶11.4

1 Complete the dialogue from the video with words from the box.

about you	happening	up to	cool	really	how

Andy: Hey Kevin. What are you ¹_____?

Kevin: Oh, I'm studying for the Latin quiz. ²_____ **about you?**

Did you study?

Andy: Nope. That's why I'm here! How's it going?

Kevin: Uhh…I'm stuck on this word. *Vici.*

Andy: *Veni, vidi, vici.* I came, I saw, I conquered. Julius Caesar!

Kevin: Ohhh!…I'm terrible at languages. So why are you taking Latin, anyway? It helps me

with science classes, but **what** ³_____?

Andy: Well, I'm thinking about law school.

Kevin: Oh, ⁴_____?

Andy: Yeah, it's good for…

Max: Hi guys. What are you up to?

Andy: Oh…We were just discussing our most important class.

Max: Oh, English?

Andy: No.

Max: Sorry. Just kidding. You were saying?

Andy: Latin 101.

Max: Oh, ⁵_____! I studied Latin in uh, "high school."

2 Choose the best response.

1 What's happening?
   a I don't like this movie.   b I'm watching a movie.

2 In Spanish class, we're reading a lot of short stories. The authors are from Argentina, and
   Colombia, and Spain…
   a Mm-hmm.   b What are you up to?

3 My favorite class is English. What about you?
   a My favorite class is math.   b I have to study tonight.

4 I'm going to study in Brazil next year.
   a Mm-hmm.   b Cool!

3 Write a conversation. Situation: You see a friend at a café. Have a conversation.

A: _____ up to? [Start the conversation.]

B: _____ [Respond. Then give the other person a turn.]

A: _____ [Respond.]

B: _____ [Listen and react. Ask a follow-up question.]

A: _____ [Answer the question. Then give the other person a turn.]

UNIT REVIEW: Podcast

Go online and listen to the podcast from the Unit Review.

1 Listen to the podcast. How is education helping to change the world? Choose the ways that the speaker talks about.

_____ 1 Education makes people more interesting.

_____ 2 Education helps people make more money.

_____ 3 Education makes people healthier.

_____ 4 Education helps the environment.

_____ 5 Education makes people happy.

2 Listen to the podcast again. Complete the sentences with the correct words.

1 Knowing how to _____ and _____ well helps people get better jobs and make more money.

2 UNESCO found that if a person has _____ more year of school, they make _____ percent more money.

3 People use this money to buy _____ and _____ for their families.

4 "Green" _____ try not to hurt the environment.

5 Education teaches people the _____ they need to get green _____.

LISTENING SKILL: Understanding the structure of a talk or radio program ▶ 11.3

3 Listen to the podcast again. What part of the podcast structure is each sentence? Choose the correct part from the box.

| conclusion | example 1 | example 2 | introduction |

Education reduces the number of poor people in the world. _____

Education is changing the world—in small and large ways. _____

So, reducing poverty and helping the environment are two ways that education is making the world better. _____

Education helps the environment. _____

DISCUSSION BOARD PREPARATION

4 Look at the Unit 11 Discussion Point. Read the questions in the prompt. Then read the reply. Does the writer agree with the quote?

_____

Unit 11 Review Discussion Point

1 Read the quote. Do you agree?
"One child, one teacher, one book and one pen can change the world. Education is the only solution. Education first."
—Malala Yousafzai, selected from *Oxford Essential Quotations*, 5th ed., edited by Susan Ratcliffe
2 How can learning change the world?
3 How is learning changing your life?

Latest: **Otto**
I agree with Malala's quote. I think that education is very important. When people have a good education, they can get a good job. Having a good job helps people to make money, and also to have an interesting life. Learning also helps people understand the world's problems better. Understanding problems makes it easier to fix them.

5 Why does the writer think that education is important?

6 Review the rubric. Use the rubric to give a score for the reply.
Give points: 0 (not successful)–10 (successful).

Writing a Discussion Board Post	Points
The post answers the questions clearly and completely.	
Sentences have subject-verb agreement.	
The post uses the present continuous correctly.	
The post uses -*ing* forms as subjects correctly.	
The post shows careful thinking about the topic.	
Sentences are complete and have correct punctuation.	
The post is long enough (50–75 words).	
Total	

WRITE YOUR POST

7 Read the quote. Do you agree? How can learning change the world? How is learning changing your life?

"One child, one teacher, one book and one pen can change the world. Education is the only solution. Education first."
—Malala Yousafzai, selected from *Oxford Essential Quotations*, 5th ed., edited by Susan Ratcliffe

8 Use the rubric from Exercise 6 to score your post. Then improve your post.

 Go online to add your comments to the discussion board.

12 Activities

Superlative adjectives ▶12.1

1 Complete the sentences with the superlative form of an adjective from the box.

long	good	big	funny	exciting

1 Alina is the _____ person I know. She always makes me laugh.

2 I think Lionel Messi is the _____ soccer player.

3 The River Palace is the _____ hotel in this city. It has 650 rooms.

4 Hong Kong is the _____ city in Asia. There's something happening all the time!

5 The Amazon is the _____ river in the world. It's 4,344 miles long.

2 Correct the mistakes in the **bold** phrases. One sentence is correct.

1 That's **the worst restaurant** in the city. _____

2 Ben is **the quieter student** in this class. _____

3 Hyde Park is **the popularest park** in London. _____

4 College was **the most happy time** of my life. _____

5 Food Mart is **the farest supermarket** from my house. _____

6 That is **the baddest show** on TV! _____

Going to: Future plans ▶12.2

3 Complete the sentences with the correct form of *be going to* and the verb in brackets.

1 I _____ a movie tonight. (watch)

2 We _____ a birthday party for my brother on Friday. (have)

3 They _____ Rome next summer. (visit)

4 Juro _____ ten people to his party. (invite)

5 My friends and I _____ games tonight. (play)

6 I _____ to ride a horse on vacation. (learn)

4 Complete the sentences with the negative form of *be going to* and a verb from the box.

have	invite	meet	play	study

1 I _____ math tonight. I'm tired.

2 They _____ soccer tomorrow. It's going to rain.

3 We _____ Amy to the party. We don't know her well.

4 She _____ up with friends tonight. She has a test tomorrow.

5 He _____ cake at his party. He doesn't like it.

Going to: Questions ▶12.3

5 Write the words in the correct order to make questions.

1 a job / she / going / is / to / get
_____?

2 they / to / ride / where / are / their horses / going
_____?

3 going / you / what / do / to / weekend / this / are
_____?

4 is / to / going / he / a soccer game / on Friday / watch
_____?

5 when / we / to / going / our grandparents / visit / are
_____?

6 Write questions with *be going to* and a verb.

1 A: What _____ do this summer?
B: I'm going to get a job.

2 A: Where _____ work?
B: He's going to work at a hotel.

3 A: _____ take a vacation this summer?
B: Yes, I am.

4 A: Why _____ stay home this weekend?
B: Because they're sick.

5 A: When _____ see your friends?
B: I'm going to see them on Sunday.

Free time ▶12.1

1 Unscramble the letters to make words or phrases.

1 G T E M E N I up with friends _____

2 making N H T G I S _____

3 riding a H E R O S _____

4 online P S I G N O P H _____

5 playing a M E A G _____

6 using social E D M A I _____

2 Match the beginning of the sentence in A with the ending in B.

A

1 Online shopping is very popular now. ___

2 Watching sports is boring. ___

3 I don't really enjoy meeting new people. ___

4 I'm scared of riding horses. ___

5 I like making things. ___

6 On Saturdays, I like meeting up with friends. ___

B

a They're so big!

b Playing them is more fun.

c Right now, I'm building a table.

d Because of this, many stores are closing.

e We usually go to a café.

f I like to spend time with two or three good friends.

Celebrations ▶12.2

3 Complete the sentences with words from the box.

birthday	holidays	invite	sandwiches
cake	ice cream	party	

1 On hot summer days, I love eating _____.

2 We're not going to have a big dinner—just _____.

3 On my _____, I'm going to have dinner at a restaurant with some good friends.

4 Rebecca always spends _____ with her family.

5 This _____ is beautiful! Who made it?

6 Why didn't Hajmil _____ Derek to his _____?

4 Choose the word that is different. Explain why using the words in the box.

foods	plural nouns	special days	verbs

1 sandwich ice cream birthday

The others are _____.

2 cake invite eat

The others are _____.

3 birthday holiday ice cream

The others are _____.

4 holidays sandwiches party

The others are _____.

VOCABULARY DEVELOPMENT: Future time expressions ▶12.3

5 Write the words in the correct columns to make future time expressions. Some words can go in more than one column.

afternoon	an hour	evening	month	year
morning	the future	three years	week	

in	next	this

6 It is now 6:00 in the morning on July 5. Put the future time expressions in order (1–8).

____ in five years ____ this afternoon

____ this evening ____ in three weeks

____ next month ____ next year

____ in two hours ____ in four months

7 Correct the mistakes in the **bold** phrases.

1 We're going to travel to China **in next summer**.

_____

2 **Next three years**, Jacob is going to finish college.

_____

3 We're going to the movies **today evening**. _____

4 **In future**, I'm going to be a chef. _____

5 The train is going to leave **on an hour**. _____

6 Luisa is going to start a new job **month next**.

_____

READING: Practice

1 Read the article. How is play the same in the early 1800s and today?

Play: Past and Present

Home | About | Articles

Over the years, play has changed. Before the early 1800s, children in the United States often worked on farms with their parents. Children and parents took breaks and played together outside.

In the nineteenth century, many adults started working for companies. Employees worked long hours, so they didn't have much time for play.

However, some children had more time for play because they didn't need to work. So companies started making board games.

Early board games were designed to teach children how to be good people. Later, games like *Monopoly* became the most popular. These games reward financial success. At the end of the game, the richest player wins!

There was a big transformation in the twentieth century. Computers quickly changed how people played. Young people started meeting up with friends less, and spending more time socializing online. Computer games were a hit with both children and adults. This is a return to the past: Adults and children like the same games, and they play them together!

—adapted from *The Oxford Encyclopedia of American Intellectual and Cultural History* by Joan Shelley Rubin and Scott E. Casper

2 Read the article again. Order the events (1–6).

_____ Children worked and played with their parents.

_____ Young people saw their friends less often than in the past.

_____ Companies made board games that taught children to be good people.

_____ People started working for companies.

_____ Adults and children started playing games together again.

_____ The game *Monopoly* became popular.

3 Read the article again. Choose *True* or *False*.

	True	False
1 In the 1700s, people usually played inside.	☐	☐
2 In the 1800s, many people got jobs with companies.	☐	☐
3 In the 1800s, children played more than they did in the 1700s.	☐	☐
4 *Monopoly* teaches children to be good.	☐	☐
5 Because of computers, people started to play differently.	☐	☐
6 Adults don't play computer games with children.	☐	☐

READING SKILL: Guessing meaning from context ▸12.1

4 Read the sentences from the article. Use context to guess the meaning of the word in **bold**.

1 Many adults started to work for big companies. **Employees** worked long hours, so they didn't have much time for play.

An **employee** is _____.
a a person who is paid to work for someone   b a person who is not a child

2 So companies started making board games. Early board games were **designed** to teach children how to be good people.

Designed means _____.
a planned and made   b interesting

3 These games **reward** financial success. At the end of the game, the richest player wins!

Reward means _____.
a to win
b to give something to someone because they worked hard or did something good

4 These games reward **financial** success. At the end of the game, the richest player wins!

Financial means _____
a connected with money   b having a lot of money

5 There was a big **transformation** in the twentieth century. Computers quickly changed how people play.

A **transformation** is a _____.
a a very big change   b an old computer

6 Young people started meeting up with friends less, and spending more time **socializing** with their friends and meeting new people online.

Socializing means _____.
a playing games   b spending time with people for fun

7 And computer games were a **hit** with both children and adults. This is a return to the past: Adults and children like the same games, and they play them together.

A **hit** is _____.
a a person or thing that is very popular   b a person or thing that is very fun

5 What words helped you guess the meaning of the word in **bold**?

Word	Words that helped me guess the meaning of the word
employee	
designed	
reward	
financial	
transformation	
socializing	
hit	

REAL-WORLD ENGLISH: Accepting and refusing invitations ▶12.4

1 Complete the dialogue from the video with words from the box.

love to	thanks for	that sounds	sorry	sure

Kevin: So if you're not busy on Sunday, I'm gonna have some friends over. You know…food, cake. And we're going to watch some baseball.

Andy: Yeah, ¹_____. What time?

Kevin: The game is at seven, but everyone's going to come at about five or six.

Andy: ²_____ great!

Kevin: Max, what about you? Can you come?

Max: Oh, I'd ³_____, but…um…I…uh…

Andy: He doesn't understand baseball.

Max: Well, you know, that's sort of true…um…⁴_____, Kevin, I just, I have my hardest, most important test on Monday morning. Art history. Yeah. I'm going to be studying all day.

Kevin: Too bad. Well, you could take a break at 8:30 and come over for cake!

Max: Ah…I don't think so. ⁵_____ inviting me, though.

2 Read the conversations. In which conversations is B polite? Not polite?

		Polite	Not polite
1	A: Do you want to come over and watch a movie tonight? B: No.	☐	☐
2	A: Would you like to play soccer with us this afternoon? B: That sounds great!	☐	☐
3	A: I'm having a little birthday party for Sylvia on Friday night. Can you come? B: Yes.	☐	☐
4	A: Do you want to go out to dinner tonight? B: I'd love to, but I have to work.	☐	☐
5	A: Hey, how about going to the beach on Saturday? B: I'm busy.	☐	☐

3 Rewrite the lines that aren't polite.

Line	Polite rewrite

UNIT REVIEW: Podcast

 Go online and listen to the podcast from the Unit Review.

1 Listen to the podcast. Answer the questions.

1 What topic are the people discussing?
   a Are you an optimist or a pessimist?   b Is it better to be an optimist or a pessimist?
2 Who thinks it's better to be an optimist?
   a the man   b the woman
3 Do the man and woman agree?
   a yes   b no

2 Listen to the podcast again. Complete the sentences with the correct words.

1 Pessimists always think the _____ thing is going to happen.

2 Pessimists are _____ happy.

3 A pessimist sees dark clouds and thinks, "Oh, no, it's going to rain! I can't _____ my friends at the beach."

4 But an optimist thinks, "A rainy day! Great! I'm going to stay home and _____ on TV!"

5 So optimists are the _____ people.

6 Optimists think things are going to be _____.

LISTENING SKILL: Understanding different voices ▶12.3

3 Listen to the podcast again. Who says each line: The host, the man or the woman?

Line	Host	Man	Woman
1	☐	☐	☐
2	☐	☐	☐
3	☐	☐	☐
4	☐	☐	☐
5	☐	☐	☐
6	☐	☐	☐

DISCUSSION BOARD PREPARATION

4 Look at the Unit 12 Discussion Point. Read the questions in the prompt. Then read the reply. Does the writer think the quote was said by an optimist or a pessimist?

_____

Unit 12 Review Discussion Point

1 Read the quote. Are these the words of an optimist or a pessimist? Why do you think so?
"Cheer up! The worst is yet to come!"
—Philander Chase Johnson, selected from the *Oxford Dictionary of Quotations*, 8th ed., edited by Elizabeth Knowles

2 Do you think it's better to be an optimist or a pessimist? Why?

Latest: **Emma**
I think these are the words of a pessimist. The person says "The worst is yet to come." This means that more bad things are going happen. I think that it's better to be an pessimist than an optimist. Pessimists are happily surprised when good things happen. But optimists have unhappy surprises when bad things happen!

5 Does the writer think it's better to be an optimist or a pessimist? Why?

6 Review the rubric. Use the rubric to give a score for the reply.
Give points: 0 (not successful)–10 (successful).

Writing a Discussion Board Post	Points
The post answers the questions clearly and completely.	
Sentences have subject-verb agreement.	
The post uses superlative adjectives correctly.	
The post uses *be going to* correctly.	
The post shows careful thinking about the topic.	
Sentences are complete and have correct punctuation.	
The post is long enough (50–75 words).	
Total	

WRITE YOUR POST

7 Read the quote. Are these the words of an optimist or a pessimist? Why do you think so? Do you think it's better to be an optimist or a pessimist? Why?

"Cheer up! The worst is yet to come!"
—Philander Chase Johnson, selected from the
Oxford Dictionary of Quotations, 8th ed.,
edited by Elizabeth Knowles

8 Use the rubric from Exercise 6 to score your post. Then improve your post.

 Go online to add your comments to the discussion board.